THE CRITERIA OF THE SHEEP

ENJOY THE WEALTH OF NOT THINKING POOR

Víctor Baptista

THE CRITERIA OF THE SHEEP

ENJOY THE WEALTH OF NOT THINKING POOR

Víctor Baptista

THE CRITERIA OF THE SHEEP

FIRST EDITION, JUNE 2020

© Víctor Baptista E-mail: Victor.blueisland@hotmail.com

Website:

Correction

Freddy Parra Jahn

Printing

THE LAWMADE

DEPOSIT LEGAL DEPOSIT ISBN 979-8639735332

The partial or total reproduction of the content of this book is prohibited without the prior and express authorization of the author.

THE CRITERIA OF THE SHEEP

Table of Contents

DEDICATION 9
CHAPTER 1 ii
THE CRITERIA OF THE SHEEP ii
    THE HERD ii
    THE BLACK SHEEP iv
    BREEDING vi
    EDUCATION viii
    TABOO MONEY x
    THE AVA RICIA xii
CHAPTER 2 xvi
BELIEFS xvi
    THE PROBLEMS REPRESENT THE OPPORTUNITIES xvi
    WITHOUT EXCUSES xviii
    DEBTS xx
    SOLUTIONS VS PROBLEMS xxii
    CONFIDENCE IN YOURSELF 25
    (THERE IS NO ONE BETTER THAN YOU FOR THIS JOB) 25
    THE MENTALITY OF THE POOR 27
CHAPTER 3 29
HABITS 29
    MANAGING TIME xxx
    WHERE YOU INVEST YOUR TIME 31
    DISCIPLINE xxxiv
    BACK, NEVER, GIVE UP xxxvi
    NO MORE DRAMA xxxviii
    DON'T LEAVE FOR TOMORROW WHAT YOU CAN DO TODAY . xl

CHAPTER 4	1
THE SOCIETY	1
THE DANGER REPRESENTED BE IN THE MIDDLE CLASS	1
ALL ARE EXPERTS	3
THE EMPATY	5
SAVING IS NOT SALVATION	7
VICTIMS OR VICTIMARIES	9
THE FEAR	11
CHAPTER 5	i
MAXIMIZE YOURSELF TO THE MAXIMUM	i
KNOWLEDGE HAS NO LIMITS	i
SALES	iii
NEGOTIATION	v
COMMUNICATION	8
FOCUS	10
THE TRIDENT OF SUCCESS	12
CHAPTER 6	lxviii
IT IS NECESSARY	lxviii
PREPARE	lxviii
ORGANIZE	lxx
EXECUTE	lxxii
PUBLICATE	lxxiv
POSITIVE	lxxvi
CHAPTER 7	lxxx
MOTIVATION	lxxx
MAKE MISTAKES YOUR FRIENDS	lxxx
BECOME AN ENEMY OF THE AVERAGE	lxxxii

THE CRITERIA OF THE SHEEP

- THINK BIG, NOW BIGGER lxxxiv
- THE RIGHT SPEED lxxxvi
- TELL ME YOUR FRIENDS, AND I'LL TELL YOU WHO YOU ARE . lxxxviii

CHAPTER 8 xc
YOU MUST BE SURE OF xc
- HE IS THE PERFECT AGE xc
- CREATING YOUR LEGACY xcii
- BE THE MOST INTERESTING PERSON IN THE WORLD xciv
- TO INFINITY AND BEYOND xcvi
- MASSIVE ACTIONS xcviii

CHAPTER 9 c
SYMPTOMATOLOGY c
- DREAMERS c
- YOU ARE DIFFERENT cii
- HUNTER OF OPPORTUNITIES civ
- LOVER OF CHANGES cvi
- CHALLENGES ARE FASCINATING cviii
- BRAVE 111

CHAPTER 10 cxiv
WELCOME TO THE BLACK SHEEP CLUB cxiv
- BREAKING CHAINS cxiv

ABOUT THE AUTHOR...cxxvi

DEDICATION

Dedicated to those who wish to open their minds and expand their horizons, to those who know that it is possible and that being successful is a universal right that is available to all, to those who understand there is nothing wrong with thinking, acting and, in general, being different, that is, for all those who want to obtain extraordinary results.

Víctor Baptista

x

THE CRITERIA OF THE SHEEP

> *"... no one is obliged to live according to the criteria of others, but each one is the guarantor of his own freedom."*
>
> **Baruch Spinoza**

CHAPTER 1
THE CRITERIA OF THE SHEEP

THE HERD
We live in a world where apparently the goal is to incite us, more and more, to think less; We always have someone telling us what we have to do and which path we have to take, even our parents, without wanting to participate in this conspiracy, transmit to us from children, with the best intention in the world, what their parents transmitted to them or what they think it's better for us. It is as if they told us: do not think, much less try, just follow your father's advice who has already gone through that stage.

We are still impressed by the modern world in which computers are becoming more and more intelligent than human beings; We do often wonder about this fact; of course, computers are and will continue to be increasingly intelligent, not only because of technological advancements but because one of the purposes of such machines is to analyze information. In contrast, the human being seems to be training to think less. Today it has become common practices for parents to give cell phones or electronic tablets to their children, only to stop running, playing, yelling, or

THE CRITERIA OF THE SHEEP

interact with other children, i.e., as the majority says: "So they stop fucking" when to screw is their nature, with this attitude we are once again transmitting to subsequent generations the idea that they do not have to think, much less interact with others.

If you don't believe it, pay attention to the children's reaction to this situation. Notice how the playful and tremendous child that you saw interacting a few minutes ago sits up and transforms, enters a kind of trance, seems to be hypnotized by some power. Showing his nature does not speak, does not give his opinion, does not make him hungry, does not make him want to go to the bathroom. As long as you have an electronic item of this type in hand with which you can access the Internet or games, we are depriving you of doing what children by nature are supposed to do, **which is fuck.**

With tools as powerful as cell phones, electronic tablets, or computers that allow us to access the Internet, which in turn gives us access to any information we know, I wonder why we do not transmit culture to our children. How to get the best out of these technological advances, how many actually take the time to teach them, and explain how to use such a source of information to their advantage.

When we get to school, practically the same thing happens, we find ourselves with an educational system in which we mainly instill the culture of not thinking; If you question a teacher, you will be in serious trouble, the culture is simple: don't think, just memorize and put such concepts on paper, this will ensure you get good grades, which in turn will guarantee you a good job in the future; I repeat: in this area it is absolutely forbidden to think, they also teach us to be in some way selfish with our companions, if it occurs to us to collaborate with any of them in a test, we are immediately accused of the great crime of examination malpractice and the immediate punishment is that we fail the exam and possibly, at the teacher's discretion, the subject; The funny thing is that in the future we do not understand why it is difficult for so many to work as a team, when the time comes to get a job the idea is easy to understand, do not think or interact, start in a job, follow instructions and you can do this way to climb positions in such a company which will take care of you when you grow old.

It is as if the system was conceived to transform thinking beings into sheep without criteria. It is a system in which you practically have to think as little as possible every day. Your life is planned by someone else since you are a child and all you have to do is follow the instructions of the pastor, whoever he is, so that things go well for you; The most interesting thing is that within these groups, a different being has been created that has been labeled as the 'black sheep', I imagine it is with the intention that the other sheep see this as a repulsive being, some kind of renegade who does not know what he wants and who the majority rejects, but they could not be further from the truth since the black sheep if something is clear, is the objective they are going to pursue.

THE BLACK SHEEP

Before continuing, it is necessary to clarify that if society labels someone as a black sheep, that does not make them a socially reprehensible individual; Let's see why by defining what a black sheep is and it's meaning to this text. Black sheep is someone who one day decides to question what comes from some kind of authority and asks society or the shepherd who leads the herd, for example: why is this our only option? or why is this our only way? Or why should we only eat what you indicate? Or why should we only be in the places that you indicate? Black sheep is nothing more than the one who one day decides to see other horizons. The one who decides to investigate what his true options are is the one who decides to venture down new paths, breaking, many times, with what is established by the system. In essence, the spirit of a black sheep lies in a proactive mentality

THE CRITERIA OF THE SHEEP

that appropriates the problems that surround society or, beyond, the world, identifying them as opportunities and taking responsibility for the risks and failures that the search for solutions.

We black sheep are nothing more than those who seek solutions to problems, those who feel the need to experience new things, who cannot see ourselves all our lives following instructions from other people, those who one day decide to fight our own battles in Instead of fighting other people's battles, there is nothing wrong with getting motivated and having the passion for going out and finding what we really want to achieve. If you so, or feel like, or want to be like, be proud, you're a black sheep.

Being different is not enough to classify a person as bad or good, in our case, we are characterized by not being afraid to take risks, we are not afraid of the unknown; rest assured that curiosity was not the one that killed the cat, there may be many other reasons, but curiosity does not kill anyone, therefore, do not be afraid of it. Just because everyone walks the same path does not mean that this is the only way to reach our destination; I invite you to let the black sheep that exists within you come out, stop thinking about all the bad things that can happen, and start thinking about all the benefits and opportunities that you could get if you decide to act differently from how others act, that is the secret. Now, suppose you want to have the same result as an average person. In that case, you just have to continue behaving like an average person and follow instructions. But, if you think you deserve a better destiny than this, this is the time to start your path to success.

Let your imagination guide you; this is how the path to success begins: an idea, some preparation and massive actions is the formula that will lead you to achieve what you want, start creating a better future for you and your family, a future without limits, without borders, in which your legacy will be as great as you want, start making your schedule, deciding what to invest your time in, not following third-party instructions, you can take the liberty of planning where and when you will enjoy your next vacation, it is time to free that being that has always been inside you, the one who has always asked you why? The one who has made you question some of your parents' recommendations, the one who has made you question, some recommendations from his teachers, that is, the one who has always questioned any authority who has tried to dictate what the way to go or tell him what the rules of the game are.

The time is now; dictate your destination, go looking for it, start working on it; by tomorrow, it could be too late. Although opportunities are present at all times and in all places, the faster you start your journey, the quicker you will arrive. Your destiny.

BREEDING
If you still have any doubts, it is perfectly understandable since the principles

that we use at the moment, have their origin in our upbringing, in the education that we receive at home and in school, and that was largely based on the instinct of protection, which by nature, parents apply to their children after the desire to keep them away from any situation that implies danger, but which was based on generationally transmitted schemes which, at that time, were the only ones that our Parents knew and assumed that they were the ones who could guarantee us a life surrounded by security, based mainly on financial security provided by a permanent, stable, comfortable job in a company that would ensure a secure future for us. Consequently, it is logical that our pre-programmed brain today is reluctant to accept or undertake something that we want to do at this time that is different from the conventional that has been instilled in us since childhood.

THE CRITERIA OF THE SHEEP

Guided by these precepts and when observing the frequent failure of many companies, it is logical to think that this is not the best path for you. For that reason, instead of encouraging us to start our own business, they encourage us to go to school to get the best grades to get a good job and thus ensure our future. This way of thinking emerged many years ago, in another era, when companies took responsibility for their employees, even after they retired; In the modern world, it no longer works this way, today companies increasingly try to move away from the idea of having some kind of responsibility once people stop working for them.

Another common situation is that of parents who encourage or encourage their children to undertake careers preferred by them or based on their own experiences. This practice is prevalent in the world of sports; the baseball fanatic father wants to encourage his son to play baseball, often even ignoring signs that your child likes other practices and is good at them, such as playing a musical instrument. It is common to see the father, accountant or doctor, doing everything possible so that his son is, equally, accountant or doctor, and this is the case with different professions or trades; once again, we can see how we are raised ignoring our will or vocation under the assumption that we must do everything our parents dictate.

It is evident that the criticisms that we have formulated regarding this form of parenting are completely beyond any doubt about the good intentions that guided our parents at such times, only that the speed with which education at home and in school is evolving. The school is not in accordance with the demands imposed by modern social dynamics, so for the achievement of what is correct, what is indicated, what is successful, it is not enough only with good intention, it is imminently necessary to act in accordance with the dynamics and the criteria imposed by modern times.

Over the years in our development as infants, we hear phrases such as: "Money does not grow on trees"; Well, if you want to be financially successful, you have to leave all these beliefs behind, money can grow in a tree if we sow the right seed, this is what cash flow is all about, we have to treat company the same as a tree. Initially, it needs a lot of our attention, that we do not forget to pour water on it, many times we need to put compost in it. But once the tree reaches its maturity, we will be able to enjoy its fruits indefinitely. However, it will always be good to give it some attention and prune it, but it will no longer need our full attention. The process of starting our own company is very similar, although there are many sacrifices that initially we will have to make in order to carry out such a project, once it grows, it will need less attention on our part, which in the long run will translate into a benefit embodied in time and money.

EDUCATION

One of the easiest ways to earn the title of black sheep is not getting good grades during their basic education. Another way is telling your family you don't have the intention to complete your schooling. If you go to college, you will most likely be awarded the title of black sheep for life. The good news for those who were never good students in school or who never, for some reason or another, finished their studies at the university is that it is no longer a secret that so many super successful entrepreneurs go through the school appeared as black sheep or that much later among relatives or society they earned this title by not attending university.

There are several reasons why many entrepreneurs do not thrive in school or show no interest in acquiring college degrees. One of the most common reasons is that modern education is focused mainly on one type of intelligence, the one who is capable of memorizing does not have to think, if you have the ability to read and remember the texts indicated by a teacher and you can put them on paper, surely you will do very well in

THE CRITERIA OF THE SHEEP

school, this definitely goes against the nature of entrepreneurs, who do not want to memorize, since by nature they are creators, they do not want to know hypothetical information, most of the business people value experiences, have an idea, and want to go out and take action to make it come true.

There are many types of intelligence, but most modern schools and universities focus on only one, perhaps they know someone who does not care what the sport is, it seems that they can play or have played all their lives, they learn them easily, and it is good for anyone who decides to practice, that is definitely a type of intelligence, the brain works in harmony with the body to create the necessary movements that an athlete needs to execute. They have met people who are very easy to learn to play different musical instruments or some who have the ability to learn several languages simultaneously, and they make it look as if it is something straightforward. All these abilities represent different types of intelligence, but most are not academically recognized.

We earn the title of black sheep because society assumes that we do not want to study, but in truth, these are far from reality; love of education is a common symptom of entrepreneurs; the difference is that we like institutional education. When we discover what we want to do, we never stop educating ourselves. We recognize, unlike others, that there are many educational paths outside the traditional or institutional ones. It is towards them that we direct our attention, we begin to read books. On the topics that interest us, we attend seminars or courses, either in person or online, that involve the subjects that interest us, today all these resources are more accessible than ever, all this, of course, thanks to the Internet. Therefore, if you are a black sheep, do not see education as an obstacle in pursuing your goals since it is not.

But not everything is bad in the modern education system. Thanks to it, we will have the best employees that the system can train since modern education is focused on creating employees and not business people like us. This is what we

pray when we form our company, people who, according to the modern educational system, can follow instructions, who are good at memorizing and applying what they have learned, in other words, soldiers willing to fight our battles on our behalf.

TABOO MONEY

Money is one of the points that deserve a deep analysis. In modern society, it seems that for some reason, people do not want to talk about money; it is as if it were a taboo, a forbidden subject. Many try to justify the lack of it with phrases such as "There are things more important than money" how we can justify a phrase like this when in modern society, everything is based on money if you do not believe it, do a brief analysis of what our day to day is. We saw a property either bought or rented, no matter what the, in any case, it is definitely not free, whether it is purchased or rented represents an expense; We need a vehicle to move from one place to another, which represents another expense, even if we do not have a vehicle, we need money to transport ourselves by other means to the places we want to go.

We live in a materialistic world where nothing is free anymore; people could build their own homes or grow their own food in another era. In modern society, their only option is to exchange money for these goods. However, health is more important than money; it does not mean that we do not need it to achieve our goals. A good diet, a fundamental aspect to achieve good health, is not free. Society, and more specifically, the middle class, based on the thesis that money cannot buy happiness, does not justify the pursuit of wealth; These are arguments directed solely and exclusively to justify a mediocre attitude protected by conformity.

THE CRITERIA OF THE SHEEP

To achieve financial success, you have to understand that happiness is within your reach but that you have to pay. I have never heard a person complaining because they have too much money, but many have told me all the problems they have for not having enough monetary resources. I have never seen someone on the street driving an exotic car with an annoyed or crying face. On the contrary, they always seem to have a smile on their face; the same happens to people who drive their own boat. It seems that the bigger the pot, the bigger the smile.

But not everything is about material things; money can bring happiness in many other ways. In my case, my father has suffered for many years from a severe illness, and the reasons why he is still alive are: on the one hand, the fighting spirit that he maintains in this situation and, on the other hand, that my sister and I have been able to help him financially to bear all the medical expenses that have been incurred to keep him alive. We definitely enjoy every minute we spend with him; it is pure happiness every minute that he can share with all the family members, especially with his grandchildren. This extra time that we have managed to enjoy has been possible, among other things, thanks to money. Although it may be true that money is not the most important thing for you, I guarantee that you will need it so that it is possible to reach that state of happiness to which you aspire, whatever it may be.

When we think about money, the best we can do is always be aware that it is a tool of freedom. It is the key that opens the doors to other opportunities, opening a million ways of possibilities that exists in abundance; To achieve financial success, you have to accept that you are a black sheep and begin to build positive beliefs about money, which will undoubtedly serve your best interests; You must be clear that it is not the lack of academic intelligence or the lack of institutional education that prevents you from achieving financial success, but fear, which, based on false beliefs originated in the middle class regarding money and success, does not allow you to take action.

THE AVA RICIA

Society never stops its attacks against those of us who evolved as black sheep. Due to false beliefs about money, we usually hear phrases such as: "You are a grateful evil, it seems that you are not satisfied with anything," but to Unlike what many believe, our species is truly grateful for everything it has, and if something is absolutely correct, it is that we are not conformists.

No reason in this world justifies the fact that we have to settle for something small; we always want more, especially financially. We are clear that when we start a trip, we will not reach a given destination on this trip. We will only be making stops. In different times and places, we ourselves are our only competition by setting an objective as a goal and fulfilling it; we do not feel satisfied. Instead, we begin to plan how we can do more.

Conformity is one of the allies of mediocrity; stop to think for a moment if you are definitely satisfied with everything you have at this point in your life if so, you will not need to seek more monetary resources or aspire to a better home, or anything to improve in your family relationships and, much less, in your social relationships, but if on the contrary, you aspire to those objectives mentioned above, you are responding to a natural nonconformity typical of the human being, and that has

nothing wrong, rather it is a symptom of wanting to excel in some or all areas of your life.

Due to this attitude, we do not settle for anything. Often, we are confused, or we are called misers. This is just another mistaken belief since all those who manage to obtain financial success always prioritize helping others. They do it through different ways, either by helping their loved ones, which may be family or friends, even beyond, sharing their wealth and time with

THE CRITERIA OF THE SHEEP

strangers, or investing part of their wealth or time in noble activities such as It can be trying to improve the world, we live in.

Changes do not come from conformist people; for this reason, the idea of conformity does not fit in our heads, or our world black sheep are innovative. We are creators, questioners. We are here to change the world. If no one questioned the authorities, there would be no changes. But the system is created with another intention: to create and raise sheep without criteria that follow instructions without questioning them, so they do not generate any problems for those who exercise authority. Conformity is a symptom of apathy which definitely goes against the nature of the black sheep; conformists develop the belief that all their problems are the fault of other people just as the responsibility to solve them belongs to other beings or entities, for For example, to the Government, they

are convinced that the Governments function as a kind of paternal or maternal figure where they not only represent authority but also have an obligation to provide everything for us, this definitely creates a conflict in the world of so-called dissatisfied, since our nature, which many qualify as rebelliousness, always leads us to ask why? It induces us to seek our own solutions instead of waiting for others to solve our problems; we are the ones who support the problem. Hand and ask; without a doubt, we are the ones who drive the changes.

There definitely many false beliefs that have been instilled in us through time. That's why we often feel pressured to take that first step because these misconceptions seem that there is an ice wall impenetrable between where we are and where we want to go when the truth is that this wall is much less thick than it appears to be. As we go through this book, you will see how such beliefs lose more and more strength, and in the end, this barrier will be so thin that with a little push, it will break the ice.

Víctor Baptista

THE CRITERIA OF THE SHEEP

> *"What we can or cannot do, what we consider possible or not possible, is rarely a function of our true ability. It is more likely a function of our beliefs about who we are."*
>
> Tony Robbins

CHAPTER 2

BELIEFS

THE PROBLEMS REPRESENT THE OPPORTUNITIES

Returning to the topic of beliefs, they are the essence of our potential. Beliefs can project or destroy us if one believes and is convinced that something is impossible, does not even try, the brain does not seek solutions to such a situation, quite the opposite happens when we convince ourselves that something is possible and that something is our objective

the brain reacts differently and immediately begins to work and analyze all the options to make this fact reality or something possible.

For this reason, we have to identify all those false beliefs that harm us. We have to eliminate those negative thoughts that end up becoming a kind of fog that does not allow us to find our way; According to this, sheep that do not develop their own criteria tend to see problems as something impossible to solve and prefer that other people take care of the situation. They do not realize that problems represent opportunities, that is, they

THE CRITERIA OF THE SHEEP

have them in front of them but do not see them. On the contrary, the black sheep see an opportunity in every problem. Thus, under this principle, they are convinced that the bigger the problem, the greater the monetary benefits derived from its solution. So this is the time to go out looking for problems, that is, opportunities, keep your eyes open so that you can identify them when they present themselves, and once you identify the problem or opportunity, prepare yourself, investigate, believe, design a work plan and take massive action, this is the only way to achieve your goals.

As a black sheep, you must definitely accept that problems, obstacles, or challenges are nothing more than opportunities. I insist on it because these situations are common in the business world, do not let them stress you, always stay objective in the search for the solution, stop seeing them as negative experiences, instead, accept them as a fundamental part of your personal development both in business and in life in general. Each problem that he manages to overcome will make him stronger. These challenges constitute determining elements for his growth, which for many represents an inconvenience. For us, black sheep, it represents a challenge that, when overcome, automatically becomes one of the strengths with which an increasingly solid base will be built on. Hence, the desired empire can be built.

The world is full of problems, great news! It means that we have an unlimited source of opportunities, but whether this reality will depend solely on your criteria, your perspective, or the way you see the world; Many of these solutions turn out to be simple as well as obvious, but in the white sheep society, nobody is looking for solutions, you are, so your mission is to identify the problem situation and get the solution, that is, turn the problem into an opportunity. Sell such a solution or innovation to that society of white sheep. Do not wait for another person or entity to solve their problems. The equation is: *problem = monetary opportunity*.

Opportunities represent the hope of improving our lives. Understanding this will leave us with no choice but to go out and look for them. Putting aside your old beliefs, your fears, or distractions, and begin your hunt for opportunities. Once that begins, we will realize that they are everywhere, and they have even been in front of us all our lives, just waiting for us to go out and take them. Any idea represents an opportunity to do something different, something new, something more, which always opens the door to new horizons. Don't wait until it's too late to ask yourself: what would have happened if…? When it comes to opportunities, you have to live your life to the fullest, take advantage of and take advantage of each one of them. Long for opportunities and never settle, because we live in a world where they have no limit. Keep in mind that the real failure lies in not trying, that is, if you do not start shooting at this point, you can be sure that you will never hit your target.

WITHOUT EXCUSES

One of the most admirable things in white sheep society is their ability to make excuses in their arduous struggle not to assume responsibilities. They have become experts in this area, the common thinking and the attitude to follow are governed by the motto: "Since the excuses were invented, no one is to blame," therefore, if at any time they feel attacked, the custom is to react and make an excuse.

The list of excuses seems endless, and they always have one at hand. It seems that the goal is to have fewer and fewer responsibilities in life, without realizing that excuses are one of the great impediments to growing and achieving achievements. What they are capable of. Excuses are nothing more than invented reasons to justify or postpone action, behavior, or simply to divert responsibility. Beyond that, they end up

THE CRITERIA OF THE SHEEP

convincing themselves that this situation is true. Therefore, it is impossible for them to assume responsibility.

Black sheep do not fear or flee from responsibility. We are not scared of making mistakes since we understand that mistakes are also made. One can learn something. We are not ashamed or afraid of change. We are not afraid of responsibility or the fact of making mistakes; in addition, black sheep understand that inventing an excuse has no other reason than to avoid responsibility. Get a car. Analysis and begin by asking yourself why you have not begun to take the necessary actions to achieve the success or financial freedom that you want so much, if when asking yourself this question, any of your answers is similar or equal to any of these: *"I don't have enough time,"* *"I don't have enough money,"* *" I am too young or, perhaps, too old to start right now,"* *" I don't know how,"* *" I don't have the training to do it,"* *" it is very dangerous,"* *"It is not easy,"* *"I am afraid,"* *"It is not the economy standard,* "*it is not the right time,* "*I do not think it will work,* "etc .; you are doing nothing but deluding yourself by postponing the achievement of your goals in this way.

Be clear that as a black sheep, you are in the obligation to start being a leader, you are obligated to take that step that will convert you from Beta to Alpha, it is time for you to change your attitude and your way of thinking, to be successful as Leader cannot continue to make excuses either for lack of action or because something did not go as planned, his focus from now on must be on the facts regardless of the situation or external circumstances, from now on your obligation is to take responsibility for the things you do and even those you stop doing when it comes to reaching your goals.

Be aware and understand that from now on, every time you make an excuse, know that you are not fooling anyone but yourself, nobody is interested in excuses, the only thing that matters in this world is the results, the results are the that they will help you move forward; So, following this idea, there are two scenarios: one, in which you are moving towards the positive, and the other, where you are stuck making excuses, we all have the power within us to achieve success; Yes, you read correctly: **"all,"** I clarify that at no time have I tried to say that it is easy if it were easy, everyone could do it.

Unfortunately, it is not easy, but something that I can assure you is that it is absolutely possible, let's stop giving our children trophies and gold medals for the simple fact of participating in a game since we are only accustoming them to not giving the best of them, we are giving the impression that no matter if they try or not, they are going to be rewarded anyway. If it were that easy, all losers would be successful. It is definitely not in this way that we want them to develop their vision or attitude in life. Let's encourage them to give their best and explain that if they give their best if they take action and do not give up, then, regardless of whether they win or lose, they can win a prize: the satisfaction that they did their best attempt because while it is true that we all have the ability to achieve success. This is only reserved for those beings who take action and persevere no matter what obstacles come their way.

DEBTS

This is another point in which the criterion of the white sheep society is very different from that of the black sheep. The difference is in how each society sees and uses the debts. In the society of white sheep, there are two positions on the issue: most of them are convinced that going into debt in order to apply the resource to recreational use justifies the fact. That is why it is that we see many receiving credit cards and immediately go shopping at a mall, or those who, based on credit, plan their vacations; In other words, the only reason they use credit is to acquire assets that depreciate over time or to spend on activities that do not help their personal or financial development; For most, this practice has become common, which can be very

THE CRITERIA OF THE SHEEP

dangerous, it is like drinking a little poison every day, at first your body will be able to assimilate that small dose, but one day you will simply not be able to take it anymore, and you will begin to suffer the consequences.

In the society of white sheep, the vast majority have never received financial education. Therefore, they cannot see how dangerous this practice can be for them. They simply use a credit card until they give no more. When this happens, the immediate solution for this group is to request another card and continue to borrow meaninglessly; it is like covering a hole by opening a deeper one. It is ubiquitous in this society that due to the exercise of this bad practice, there comes a time when the debt is so extremely large that they cannot meet it.

There is also a group in this society that maintains that getting into debt is the worst thing that can be done. They see debt as an evil that they do not want to suffer from. Every time one of these individuals approaches me and manifests that they feel proud for not having debts, my question is always the same: why? And the reaction is always very similar. Firstly, they see me as if I had two heads and, then, they start with the same story, the same tone, and the same attitude of disbelief. They do not understand why I do not share with them the concept that debt is evil.

Let's clarify, in principle, that the debt is not bad or good; what gives it one or the other meaning is the use we give it. It is like a sharp knife that a cook can use as a tool to make the most dishes. Exquisite, in that case, the use that is given to that knife is good, but if the same knife is used to harm another person or even oneself, then the use that has been given to that same knife is wrong. It is bad. In the black sheep society, it is clear that debt is not bad as long as it is used in a good way. There are many scenarios where debt can be used in that sense, such as applying it to acquire goods that will increase their value in the future.

Why not ask for a commercial loan to start or expand your business? This debt, without a doubt, would be giving you the power to increase your potential in stoneware. Black sheep understand that the great benefit of leverage comes from debt, a concept that we will talk about at length later; This does not mean that you run away at this time to get into debt to acquire assets, even in a society of black sheep, some prefer to stay away from debt, my intention is that you understand that if the debt is used consciously with the intent to acquire assets this fact can definitely generate great benefits in your favor.

Another area where debt is justified is in education. Although it is not considered an asset, I consider it the most important asset; To be successful, you must prepare yourself, and there is no better way to achieve this than by educating yourself. Of course, without losing sight of what was established when we spoke earlier about this topic. I am not referring to traditional education. I am referring to the education that will truly guide you through the course you want to take. You do not need a university degree. If your desire is to obtain a degree, do it, but be aware that today's financial success does not depend on that. What is mandatory is to educate yourself in different areas. This will always incline the scales in your favor.

SOLUTIONS VS PROBLEMS

Now, let's talk about the problems. Regardless of race, religion, gender, age, or other characteristics, no one lives a life without problems. They are present in the daily lives of all people. But how these problems are faced makes a difference that depends on which of the two societies we have been talking about these people belongs to.

Let's see: those of the white sheep society, having a personal problem, tend to exaggerate the magnitude of it to the maximum, running from one place to another and letting everyone know how unfortunate they are for the fact that they

THE CRITERIA OF THE SHEEP

are going through such a situation, they focus all their attention on the problem but, as we pointed out previously, without the intention of looking for a solution to it. On the other hand, those who militate in the society of black sheep when dealing with a problem. They make use of the immense power of the mind and focus all their attention on one thing: analyzing the event, directing all their energy to the different ways in solving the problems.

They take charge of the situation; In other words, if you focus your energy on the problem, it is most likely that you will be filled with negative thoughts and, as a consequence, you will be a victim of fear, doubt, or thoughts that will not allow you to move forward. On the other hand, if you concentrate on finding solutions, your brain will automatically activate and begin to work logically, increasing the chances of achieving positive results. Take the time to analyze the situation by concentrating only in finding solutions carefully. This will help you stay on track in your search for such answers.

To be successful in both business and life, you need to start making this practice a habit as you can be sure that most problems don't solve themselves, so instead of sitting around waiting for someone else Look for a solution to a problem situation, start to see this as your obligation and in this way, you will always be willing to face problems with a positive attitude. Furthermore, if you focus formally on solving the problem rather than on how bad or serious the situation is, you will find that you can deal with the problem without much trouble; This practice is essential if you want to go from white sheep to black sheep; This change in favor of how to behave in such situations will definitely bring positive results both in your personal life and in business.

As we have said before, each problem represents an opportunity that translates into valuable experiences in your personal and business development. No matter how big the problem looks, it will lose all the negative energy that could ever affect him once you get the solution. By making this practice part of your daily life, you will begin to feel the desire to improve all the things that surround you, white sheep specialize in pointing out problems, but black sheep is characterized by being the ones who seek and achieve solutions.

How many times have you encountered the same problem? As long as you do not solve it, be sure that it will continue to be a problem in your life. But once you find the solution, it will lose its importance and will have become an opportunity. Now, project the consequences positive chances of having solved that problematic situation that presented itself think that it is possible that there are other people, like you, going through the same thing, at this point, you would have the excellent opportunity to share that solution with those others and, even more, even it is possible to get a financial benefit in return. This is just one of the many advantages that result from changing our criteria of where to focus our energy when we have a problem.

Since we are talking about problems and solutions, let's seize the moment and do a little theoretical exercise, starting with the fact that a person dared to buy a book entitled "Learn to think like a business person"; If we asked him: how do you feel about what you have read ?, you will have two possible answers: the first, he will say that he feels good and understands the content, in this case, definitely the black sheep that is already inside that reader He took over, which really brings joy and makes him a good candidate for the black sheep club; the second, he does not feel comfortable with what he has read and is confused by many of the presented in that book. If this is the case, he definitely has a problem, and that is that the white sheep inside him is still in control. He can then do one of two things: firstly, stop reading the book and continue living his life the way white sheep live. Now, if you really want to go ahead and make changes in his life,

THE CRITERIA OF THE SHEEP

he must choose the second option, that is, finish the reading without stopping. In this way, he will be forced to free the black sheep and open his mind to new ideas, to new horizons, putting into practice what these ideas presented; you can start writing your destination with the complete assurance that it will be full of great things. By doing that, We will welcome you, and we assure you that you will not be alone on the road to success.

CONFIDENCE IN YOURSELF
(THERE IS NO ONE BETTER THAN YOU FOR THIS JOB)

At this point, I can deduce that the black sheep inside you has already been completely liberated or, at least, that you are in the process of taking control; Whatever the case, I am extremely proud that you have made such a decision, and I believe that there is no one better for this job than you, and like me, you too must be convinced of that. It's time to grow your self-esteem, to start to trust yourself. If someone calls you arrogant, feel good about it as white sheep confuse confidence with arrogance. To reach your highest potential, you are obligated to be a leader, which means that others follow you as you show them the way.

Therefore, it is essential that you start to believe in yourself as this is the only way for others to believe in you, start to value your opinions, maintain your positions, and let your judgment help you make the best decisions, observe To those who achieve success, see how these individuals radiate incredible confidence when they speak or act, this confidence comes from the fact that they definitely believe in themselves and what they are doing and thus transmit it to other individuals, but do not know. Confused, the confidence they have in themselves is not due to their success; their confidence in themselves came first, which was precisely what prompted them to get where they have arrived.

Self-confidence is crucial since it is the fulcrum that will allow you to achieve any goal you set for yourself in life. If self-esteem has not been your strong suit so far, do not worry, that is something that you can work on and improve every day. You will definitely need the confidence to face new challenges. Those who do not trust themselves are usually overcome by fear and insecurity. That is why they prefer to stay in the 'comfort zone,' which is the area where they feel comfortable without taking risks. One of the consequences of this life is staying stuck in the same place without even trying to outdo yourself. Trusting yourself will help you understand how powerful you are and allow you to deal with frequent destructive comments and criticisms in competitive areas without negatively affecting you.

Self-confidence is the source of objectivity and strength that will help you cope with problems and keep you from backing down. Even when the white sheep around you repeatedly tell you that what you are trying to do is impossible. Trusting yourself and maintaining your position is extremely important when it comes to doing something that most consider being unattainable; If there is not enough self-confidence, your self-esteem will not be substantial, and this could seriously undermine it in an environment where criticism, comparison, false expectations, and false beliefs, among many other negative aspects, will be continually haunting you with the purpose to end their intentions.

It is a sad reality that many times our environment does not constitute a healthy environment for personal development since the attention of some is focused on attacking to end the positive actions of others, this position for them is, for some reason, easier and more pleasant to adopt than other constructive attitudes that could be practiced at that moment. However, before this, there is the level of confidence that the black sheep generally have. They have a high mind level, and that level is what you should aspire to, but you have to have enough confidence to make and execute your own decisions to get there. After all, only two things can happen once you have decided to

THE CRITERIA OF THE SHEEP

do something. On the one hand, it could turn out that you did the right thing, which will help you move forward on your path, but on the other, it could be that you made a mistake. This has nothing wrong since there is as much to learn from the mistakes made as from the right decisions. Whatever the result of your decision is, it will always be contributing to your personal development.

THE MENTALITY OF THE POOR

This is a highly controversial issue, so we will try to be objective about it: we live in a world where we all have the same opportunities, how many know or have heard from people who, in one way or another, started from scratch, having nothing, without meeting anyone or without any academic education but who in one way or another managed to achieve financial success in life; If these people could achieve it, how is it possible that others cannot? To the mind, I think that definitely, the mental state a person is in affects his reality, at the moment that an individual thinks that something is impossible, in his world it will be impossible; If you think it is unattainable, in your world it will be unattainable, whatever excuse you put on your head, it will end up becoming your reality, I imagine that this is where the famous saying comes from that each head is a world.

The vast majority in white sheep society cannot advance because their reality does not allow it. Therefore, they do not even try, and they live in a scarce world where everything is limited, including opportunities. Communities these limitations end up stagnate these individuals, convincing them that this is the best thing they can do or have in life. There is nothing better for them, and that it is better that they settle for what they have. Conformity is one of the most dangerous areas in which a person can be since in that world there is no intention to overcome, many tend to make the mistake of staying in this reality forever, this is the world of the poor or, the mentality of the poor, I am convinced that such a mentality has nothing to do with the purchasing power of a person but rather with their way of thinking, that is, with the reality they live. In the world of conformity, the middle class is the largest population. These low-income people decide one day to break the chains of conformity. When they reach the middle class, they fall back into that state of conformity. They convince themselves by saying that they have already risen a step in the social levels and that that is enough. It is extremely easy to get caught up in this reality.

There is an immense population of conformist beings on our planet. Those who live in this reality already consider it an outstanding achievement to reach this status. I have nothing against those who reach this level. I congratulate them as long as they understand that this is only a stop and not their destination, as long as they understand that beyond what they are living at this moment, there is much more.

So if poverty has to do with a mental state marked by conformity, in which fear prevails, lack of initiative, where there is no type of ambition, where there is no conviction that there are possibilities of arising, where beings who live this reality are convinced that this is the best they can have in their lives, a reality in which credit is used only and exclusively to acquire liabilities, among many other negative aspects, then there are as many or more individuals, locked in the mentality of the poor in the middle class than in the low-income class.

From now on, when in this book we talk about poverty, we will be referring to the mental state of a person or the reality where he lives, which has nothing to do with his purchasing power,

It is even more common than it is believed that close relatives of people who have achieved financial success live happily in this reality. This is due, I imagine, to the absence of needs. They settle for what they have, which leads to not trying to move forward in life. This state of conformity and not wanting to do anything to improve in life is what I consider the mentality of the poor.

A poor person is defined in the dictionary as one *"who does not have what is necessary to live or who has it with scarcity"*; understand that poverty is a reality that many live, but being born or being poor in a moment of our lives does not mean that we have to live forever in that world of scarcity when I speak of the mental suchness of the poor I mean the mentality of conformity, if you settle for being poor, then you will be poor all your life; If you settle for being middle class, this will be your reality and you will be in this situation your whole life; Even the person who reaches a certain financial level and is satisfied with what he has at the moment can be seduced by conformism and stop moving forward in his life. No to success and personal improvement never ends. They are just levels that we are reaching and exceeding, but there will always be one more level to reach. In this sense, there will always be space, no matter our purchasing power, to advance and improve both in the personal and financial areas.

"We are what we repeatedly do. Excellence, then, is not a act; It is a habit."

Aristotle

CHAPTER 3
HABITS

MANAGING TIME

As a black sheep, you have to learn both to value and manage your resources in the best possible way to get the most out of them, there are many you will have, but at this point, we will talk about the most valuable: time, of all assets or resources that it has, this is the only one that is considered limited, hence the great importance of knowing how to manage something so precious.

Time does not discriminate. Regardless of your financial availability, you will never be able to acquire more than it. There are 60 seconds in every minute, 60 minutes in every hour, 24 hours in every day, and so on; everyone, whatever our conditions. We have the same time, the same hours, minutes, and seconds. So how is it possible that many can manage their time so well that it seems that they do in one day what many others take a week to do? The great secret is in good time management. This is the only resource that, regardless of the society to which it belongs, what the beliefs or criteria are, we all receive it in equal amounts.

Time is often not given the importance it deserves. Perhaps this is the most overlooked resource, if you ask some people to make a list of the most important things, most will refer to family, friends, health, physical condition, which are the most popular, but in very few lists you will see time mentioned, the importance of time for many goes unnoticed, they do not acknowledge that lost time can never be recovered, you cannot make time grow to have more or, buy it, and from there comes the great importance of knowing how to manage it wisely.

Start to use your time wisely in important, enjoyable activities, and that leaves you some kind of benefit. If you do not know where to start, make a list of your daily activities and what you dedicate to each of them, you may be surprised that you waste on activities that have no meaning in your life; This will allow

THE CRITERIA OF THE SHEEP

you to organize yourself and determine how much of your valuable time you are willing to invest in them. Keep in mind that no one can tell you how to spend your time. You are solely responsible for managing it. Starting your day without goals and any kind of objective is one of the worst things you can do if you are trying to manage your time efficiently; We all have our own responsibilities and priorities, and creating a universal to-do list and a single method to do it is almost impossible. Still, we can use a methodology by applying simple planning guidelines that allow us to do so.

Miter the use or allocation of our time strategically according to the importance we assign to the goals that we set for ourselves on a daily basis. Successful people plan their day aware of the importance of time. Planning your day necessarily implies appropriately distributing your time. Once you have your list of all the things you need to do in the day, determine the importance of those activities and the time you should invest in each of them, this will lead you to establish priority; Following this idea, the activity that has the highest priority has to be at the top of your list and so on according to their importance. Do your best to finish one task before starting the next. This will give you better results. Always do your best to complete your activities in the time allotted for them.

WHERE YOU INVEST YOUR TIME

Now that we have a clearer vision of the importance of time, we can identify some of the most common areas where we usually invest our valuable time without any sense. With this look ahead, we will have the ability to identify areas in which we waste time by engaging in activities that do not provide us with positive benefit in return, one of the most common places where the vast majority invest a high percentage of their time is on television. I recommend staying away as much as possible from it, especially the news they transmit, but staying informed is also extremely important. I suggest that you search the net for news that is really of interest to you instead of filling up with negative information, which is what the news unfortunately sells today, it does not matter if it is the morning news, the afternoon or the night, the usual thing is to present spaces full of drama and negative situations that somehow keep you waiting for the outcome of those stories, which undoubtedly represents a great distraction since it will end up taking them away from their objectives and diverting their attention towards aspects that will not give you anything positive. The same happens with programs of the genre of novels. The effect that these programs cause never ceases to amaze. It is as if they had the power to hypnotize the viewer, creating a kind of addiction to which they must go daily to come back for more.

In addition to having television, we also have access to the Internet in the modern world, which has evolved as a double- edged sword. On the one hand, it is one of the ways through which endless benefits can be obtained for you. As for your business, but, on the other hand, it can be one of the most dangerous traps when we talk about wasting time; it is full of distractions, unnecessary publicity, and empty information, among other aspects, whose sole intention is to attract the attention of those who surf the net, which leads them to invest or waste their precious time doing empty activities; one of these dangerous areas is constituted by the so-called networks

If used intelligently, they can generate innumerable benefits for you, but in them, it is very easy to miss the path and end up as a majority, investing a large part of time, which could be productive, in activities that will not leave you anything positive, such as games or, simply be aware of what happens in the lives of others.

We live in a world where your approach will constantly be tested, distracting yourself and stopping working on your proposed goal seems to be a common practice in modern society, distractions

THE CRITERIA OF THE SHEEP

are becoming more and more accessible, and somehow way they have increased the power that they exert on their victims, becoming an irresistible temptation, always be alert and attentive to where or in what you are investing your time, ask yourself before starting an activity, what benefit will I get from this act? Time investing, perhaps the most valuable and least recoverable of the resources you possess.

Have you ever heard it said that "life is not a race, it is a marathon"? I totally agree with that. Let's see together how I interpret this magnificent metaphor: when we talk about a race, we refer to a generally short route, and nobody aspires to a short life, we desire to live a long, and above all, a productive life that is what we have been talking about, that is why we must associate it with a marathon. But be careful! In the marathon, because it is a long journey, with many distractions around (people, landscapes, other corridors, etc.), if you are not concentrated and focused on your goal, your pace may drop when paying attention to that environment, fatal mistake!

In your marathon, in your actions as a long-distance runner, as an entrepreneur, as a black sheep that you are, you cannot be looking to the sides, nor slowing down, there is not the future to which you should aspire, you cannot lose your time in distractions, it does not depend on anyone but yourself the form and speed at which you decide to compete in such a race since you are its pilot and, therefore, the one in control of the machine, it is about always maintaining and controlling what you do, don't let distractions divert you from your path. Always keep a list of your priorities handy, which will map your path to achievement; to be able to invest your time as much efficiently as possible, it is important that you are clear about the difference between being busy and being productive, most white sheep live busy but without producing any extra benefit in their lives, do not fall into this trap, try to ensure that your time is always producing some benefit.

The goal is to produce the greatest benefits through the proper use of your time. When I refer to benefit, I do not solely mean the monetary aspect since there are many other benefits apart from money. It could be an experience that we leave some knowledge. Stay focused and focused on your goals and priorities, learn to say no! to distractions even coming from close people such as family and friends, try to create or strengthen the good habit of discipline every day until making it a common practice that will lead you to the achievement of your goals.

DISCIPLINE

In the development of your life as a black sheep, discipline is a habit that you can never afford to stop practicing. Although motivation is an element that plays a vital role in achieving your goals, discipline will help you on the journey. It will give you the power to carry out your tasks regardless of your feelings or mood. It does not matter if you are tired or if you think it is not the right time since you are sad because your favorite team lost a game. The Discipline is that magnificent force that will push you to do what you have to do.

Being clear about the vital importance of the little time we have (remember that it is not infinite) and how important it is to comply with all the projects that we have established as priorities, taking action and being disciplined is the only way by which we will achieve move a little further every day on the long road to success; disciplined action is what will allow us to ignore all the distractions and temptations that exist in our environment with the intention of diverting our attention to empty activities that have nothing to do with the fulfillment of our objectives.

Developing the good habit of discipline will create a unique and fundamental skill that can ensure great achievements in the course of your life. It is about the ability to work every day to achieve your goals. Discipline is an art, and your mission is to integrate it definitively into your life. The interesting thing about

THE CRITERIA OF THE SHEEP

habits is that they do not discriminate or limit themselves. This means that you can practice any and as many you want regardless of your economic situation, age, sex, or other characteristics that you have. Habits are only a resource, a personal tool oriented to how we will face the day-to-day in our lives. For many black sheep, having achieved success is a product of the discipline they managed to develop in the course of their lives. Even for some, it was more important than the skills or knowledge they had to achieve their goals.

Discipline is a common factor in achieving success in many areas of life. Suppose you question business people, artists or athletes, among others, about what are or were the skills that most influenced their victories and triumphs. In that case, I guarantee you that everyone will have discipline on their list as one of the fundamental elements in the successful development of their careers. Something that I find interesting and curious is how the white sheep created in their society their own concept of discipline and consider it as something impossible to develop or only applicable to small groups such as, for example, the military; this society associates this good habit with limiting and being restricted with himself in the pleasures of life. On the other hand, black sheep use different criteria and understand that this good habit can be developed and practiced by anyone and that it represents strength and self-control, which, without a doubt, is a fundamental tool that can and should be counted on if we want to take control of our lives and determine the course we want to follow.

New generations in white sheep society have specialized in applying the habit of procrastination, and it has become customary to substitute discipline for anything that needs discipline; As we already know, the list of excuses that this group has is endless, and when they have to work on any of their priorities they go to this list and convince themselves that it is okay to leave it for later, that is, to postpone it, well either because it's late, or because they are tired, or because it is the weekend and there are other things to enjoy these days that are more important than those we have to do every day to improve. Unfortunately, it seems that the new generations do not know how to say no to anything and, therefore, they easily fall victim to whatever distraction comes their way.

This is the time when you should stop procrastinating and instead start executing discipline may be the factor you need to adopt to separate and differentiate yourself from the majority of the population and become part of a select few. A group made up of those who are characterized by being successful in life. It is time for them to understand that without discipline, it will be challenging to achieve their goals and, even if they do, it will be temporary, making it almost impossible for them to stay at this level. As a result, you will have wasted your limited and precious time in life. It is not always about following the most beautiful, the brightest, or the easiest. With the exercise of discipline, you can become that artist who sees a stone, visualizes a work of art in it, and will have the patience to work with perseverance and perseverance day by day in this sculpture until obtaining the product that he wanted in the beginning.

BACK, NEVER, GIVE UP
We are going to dedicate this point to talk about perseverance and the importance it has in the development of your life as a black sheep; their presence is decisive for the achievement of maximum efficiency when it comes to achieving or satisfying the priorities that we have established for ourselves. If we want to be black sheep and achieve the desired successes, it is mandatory to start practicing it immediately; constancy is one of the fundamental factors to achieve success, to be passionate. Doing or doing what you like is not enough, even doing something that we like, we also have to put our efforts to be disciplined and thus cultivate the virtue of taking actions constantly, that is, being constant; In principle, everything that we can achieve by

THE CRITERIA OF THE SHEEP

combining and putting into practice all these factors is often underestimated. But by mastering these practices, there are no limits, and the results that can be obtained will be surprising even for yourself.

Consistency has to do with completely surrendering to priority activities, that is, staying fully committed to such tasks and turning away from all distractions. Therefore, being constant requires a commitment on your part, since this is an effort of action maintained continuously and focused in the long term to achieve what was proposed and thus go forward every day, for as long as necessary, until reaching your goals. Constancy means not stopping, not giving up, not backing down. It is about focusing on the present moment to achieve a long-term goal or vision. Unfortunately, not being constant will lead to a state of stagnation in which it will not only be very difficult to move forward. But it will be more and more challenging to get out of this situation since old and bad habits tend to take control in this state. We know this state as deferral, and it is one of the favorite places for the white sheep. Therefore, I recommend that you stay as far away from this area as possible. The struggle between stagnation and advancement will always be present in your life.

To be successful, you have to keep moving constantly. There is no secret formula, or achieving success is something magical. To achieve the goals, you just have to start applying basic fundamentals and developing good habits. One of these basic fundamentals is represented by constancy, and the best thing about this is that everyone is the fundamentals and good habits are available to anyone. That is, they are available to anyone who wants to go out and claim them as their own, apply them and develop them continuously.

I am sure that you have heard the phrase *"practice is what makes perfect."* However, I think this phrase lacks the adjective 'constant,' since what leads us to develop our maximum potential is to practice and take action constantly. It is only by acting in this way that we could consider ourselves masters in the area; by doing so, we end up being what we constantly do. In this way, habits are created, and it is the continuous practice of these good habits that leads us to excellence or, in that case, to become masters of it. It is the constancy that gives the incredible power to the water to defeat or mold the stone. Likewise, being constant will give it the necessary power to overcome any obstacle in your way, no matter how big it looks. Discipline is what gives rise to perseverance; the practice of these good habits will lead us to a state of continuous progress; at this point, we will not pay attention to the distractions that surround us. I will not be more than ever, at the mercy of doubt or fear. There will be neither drama nor excuses to stop us from advancing on our way.

NO MORE DRAMA
Now suppose that you are faced with the dilemma of doing or not doing, starting or staying in the same place. You doubt whether to advance in the path of the black sheep or to follow the path of the white sheep, that is, your life at this moment is full of all the drama created by the excuses coming from fear to justify not taking action, of that fear that constitutes the greatest reason why the white sheep prefer to stay in their world of conformity and not give the first step towards different paths full of possibilities. That fear usually works as a magnifying glass that amplifies negative things, giving the impression that an obstacle is something extremely large and solid. Therefore, impossible to overcome; that is what paralyzes the vast majority and does not allow them to advance at a given moment in their lives. It is a general evil that can affect both white sheep and black sheep. No group is truly safe from fear, and it is like if it were stalking us all the time and waiting for the defenses to be down to attack and seize one. It is more common than you think, so much that, even a black sheep, after having passed certain obstacles and having reached Certain goals, are attacked

THE CRITERIA OF THE SHEEP

by the fear of losing everything that has been achieved so far, can resign and decide to stagnate in the place where it is at that moment.

No society is immune to fear because it evolved in us as a basic survival mechanism that is activated in the face of a threat of danger. Based on this, we have that fear can be used in our favor since it allows us to recognize some dangerous situation, so it must be clear that the problem is not being afraid since it is part of us, what must be done is to learn to face it for our benefit. For example, in the past, it could happen that in the face of imminent danger of being attacked by a predator, the best option was to flee the area as quickly as possible or, on the contrary, to remain immobile in the hope that said predator would not see you. Today, in the modern world, these reactions are obsolete since this mechanism is activated most of the time; it is not because our life is in danger, but rather it is due to other circumstances. So, what are we really afraid of right now?

One of the most common triggers is the fear of the unknown. Not even black sheep, after acquiring certain levels of success, is so exempt at some point from being afraid of the unknown. Keep in mind that you can have access to almost any information you want to acquire in the modern world. If something is unknown to you, it does not mean that it is bad. Obtain the necessary information about it in order to take the necessary actions and in this way continue to move forward. When you feel afraid, the worst thing you can do is do nothing, act! Even if no one guarantees that it will have positive results and that it will be an easy job, do not deny yourself the opportunity to start the journey to a world full of possibilities. Do not limit yourself because of fear, personal development, and much less financial development.

If the trigger comes from the fear of failure, it means that you are a victim of one of the false beliefs formed in the white sheep society. I mean something planted within us since we were very young; when we are in school, failing a test means something bad, and we are generally punished or questioned for this failure. Well, it is time to free yourself from this false belief since, as a black sheep, you must understand that there is nothing wrong with making mistakes since even mistakes can result in positive experiences from which we can learn many things. The point I want to reach is that if you can identify the source or the trigger that triggers that fear, it will be much easier to face it instead of ignoring it; prolonging or leaving your priority activities for tomorrow is an attitude that we have to avoid at any time in our lives. Therefore, the time to do something is today; you just have to find the strength or courage to take the first step.

DON'T LEAVE FOR TOMORROW WHAT YOU CAN DO TODAY

The creation and development of a good action system are what will allow us to be productive and keep in continuous progress as long as we are responsible and commit ourselves to apply it, not only is it enough to become a black sheep and wish for changes in your life, you have to go out to find them, face them and execute them, and the smartest way. How to do it is by being disciplined. This is the only way to achieve what they are looking for and maintain their achievements. We already know that by being disciplined, we develop the good habit of perseverance, which will help us fight against those evils that are lurking at all times, such as fear. Having understood that the problem is not to be afraid but how to face it and that by being disciplined and constant, fear will have less force on us.

Now we will talk about another of the very common evils in the society of white sheep, and of which black sheep can sadly become victims, that is to say, that even by becoming a black sheep, you will be immune to this disease called procrastination, this is known as the fact or bad habit of delaying or postponing

THE CRITERIA OF THE SHEEP

activities or situations that must be addressed, replacing those with others that turn out to be more irrelevant or more pleasant.

Knowing that in the society of white sheep generally, they tend to evade responsibilities and have no interest in advancing due to conformity. It is not difficult to understand why they are extremely vulnerable to this evil. It is very common that every time they have an important activity in front of them, they decide to ignore it or put it aside and postpone it for another occasion. The interesting thing is that the black sheep is not immune to this disease, which means that it can be attacked and harmed by it at any time.

Due to their nature as creators, Black sheep always have ideas, developing projects, tasks, systems, among many other activities in which they participate. But since it is not only about doing things but about doing the most important or priority things, It is more common than you think that a black sheep suffers from procrastination. Unconsciously, since trying to do everything can fall into the trap of starting to postpone some priority activities and replace them with others that are more important but that they really are not; As a result of this, it stagnates or progresses very slowly, the worst thing is that when entering this state, sometimes because of being so busy, the victims do not usually realize the evil they are suffering which can have extremely serious consequences in the fulfillment of its objectives. This is a silent killer who is always on the lookout for sheep without discriminating their criteria and represents one of the greatest enemies for those who seek success in different areas of life.

As a black sheep, you will have countless activities, ideas, tasks, or projects to do, some more fun, more interesting, or more promising than others, but these characteristics are not what will allow you to establish which of all these activities, ideas, tasks or projects must be the first to be attended to, it is vitally important that their activities are developed according to their priority nature, that is, due to the importance, they have in relation to the fulfillment or achievement of their objectives. We are aware that there are many reasons why you may decide to postpone an important activity, so it is highly recommended that you always keep your goals and priorities close at hand as a reminder of how closely important they are in achieving your goals. These are the activities that deserve more time on your part. Stay away from the distraction. The new chapter of your favorite novel should not be a reason why your development or growth should be stopped; it seems that more and more the distractions that have led the sheep, regardless of their criteria, to postpone priority activities for them, therefore, throughout your career you must be aware of not being a victim of procrastination, stay at all times measuring your progress and reviewing your list of priorities. However, there is no antidote to this evil. This is one of the best ways to be as far away from it as possible and stay focused on what is truly important.

> "Nature has made man happy and good, but society depraves him and makes him miserable."
>
> Jean-Jacques Rousseau

CHAPTER 4

THE SOCIETY

THE DANGER REPRESENTED BE IN THE MIDDLE CLASS

In the middle class, we get the largest population of white sheep in existence: the largest number of conformism beings who, in one way or another, do not intend to advance in their lives, at least when we refer to the area. Financial; many white sheep that belong to the lower classes in the financial sphere transform into black sheep motivated by the desire to improve themselves, but a large number of those who manage to climb a few steps to reach the much-desired middle class tend to let the white sheep within them take control, as a consequence, they end up losing the spirit of improvement and settle for having only achieved something and this something they consider sufficient. In the society of white sheep that belong to the middle class, many times, there is a false sense of pride. Many develop an enormous ego that leads them to believe that they are superior in their world to the groups with less capacity. Acquisitive than they enjoy and are also full of what they believe are justifications but are only excuses to hide why they cannot exceed this level.

These groups live in a limited world, not realizing that the potential growth of their income begins with their way of thinking and their attitude in life, that most limitations do not come from external forces but from internal forces. that the overcoming of a being, and especially in the financial area, does not depend on anyone but himself; If you do not understand these principles it is because you are thinking like a white sheep and as such I guarantee that you will never be able to understand why black sheep use this criterion, that is, you will never understand how they think and much less how this group acts, which uses criteria Such as that financial success is not achieved only through a good idea, beyond that, it has to do with the thought and actions that we apply in our day to day life.

The financial criteria used by the white sheep society are based on a world of scarcity. With this, they justify the impediments that, according to them, exist and that do not allow them to overcome their economic situation. The popular belief in this society is that wealth is a privilege for a lucky few. This is one of the worst mental states in which a being can be. On the contrary, the black sheep, motivated by their spirit of self-improvement, regardless of the economic situations they find themselves in or the level in which society has placed them, understand that money is not scarce. Therefore, they always want more money.

White sheep, in their part, are convinced that riches are for beings more intelligent than themselves. In contrast, the black sheep is clear that riches are not assigned to the most intelligent but are wisely earned by those who are better prepared. In addition, they are convinced that making and earning money is something simple that anyone can achieve. At the same time, the white sheep are convinced that making money is very complicated and very difficult. Possibly because the only way they know and apply to make money is wrong to invest your precious time.

The middle-class lives in a world of conformity and scarcity. For this reason, white sheep tend to develop only and exclusively

THE CRITERIA OF THE SHEEP

negative thoughts. This is a perilous state in which they can fall, as this form of thinking is determined by how they see and cope with situations. Facing a situation full of negative thoughts can create the illusion that it is an insurmountable obstacle and therefore conclude that it is not worth even trying to overcome it. But this very situation faced with a positive perspective will present itself to us as an opportunity since, for positive thinking, there are only possibilities and opportunities. For no reason, a black sheep faces a situation thinking that it is impossible to overcome.

The white sheep belonging to the middle-class social group, absorbed by that world where an atmosphere of negativism prevails, find it difficult to do something new that they no longer even try it, therefore, if they wish, and I mean you! ! is to get out of the vicious circle of conformism in which most white sheep live, at this moment you must change your way of seeing and dealing with things. Authorize yourself to be different because if you act like the great majority, you will have the same results as them. The group made up of the so-called middle class is extremely large. There is something that seems curious and interesting about them, is that they all believe they are experts. Whatever subject you intend to practice or apply, they are not afraid to demonstrate their knowledge whatever the subject, but since they live in a world where negativism predominates, this is exactly what they will convey to you when they think about what you want to do. So be very careful when deciding who to pay attention to, since listening to the wrong person may give up before trying because you are a victim of the negativity they can transmit.

ALL ARE EXPERTS

In a world whose population is predominantly made up of white sheep, we have to be extremely selective when consulting or listening to someone's opinion. It is common to hear opinions not based on solid knowledge on the subject but rather based only on the reality in which the one who expresses such an opinion lives. One way to check this is as follows: just comment, in a group, that you suffer from some simple sickness. For example, a sore throat, so you can see if anyone has the cure for such a disease, you will hear different opinions on the best way to attack this situation. Suppose this is the case and your throat hurts. In that case, my recommendation is that you consult a doctor and do not listen to all those who think they know about medicine and are not qualified to diagnose it, much less to recommend the appropriate medication. It is common that when you have the initiative to do something new, such as starting your own business, the white sheep that surround you, by their negative nature, try to convince you that this is definitely a bad idea, and that opinion usually comes from those who have not had even tried to start their own business and therefore have no experience in the matter.

It is your obligation, from now on, to always be alert regarding who decides to listen; When it comes to opinions and advice to follow, it is vital to pay attention to those who come solely and exclusively from experts in the field and not from some of the many naive that exist in the world and that they try to sell your ideas based on the criteria and fears that they handle and that generally have nothing to do with you. Although it may be that the opinions come from family members or very close friends, this does not mean that they express their opinions with the intention of doing you any harm. On the contrary, they do so with the best possible intention and are convinced that this is their best option. But the intention does not make them experts. Therefore, it is important to rate the person before applying such advice or opinions.

It seems that the balance tips every time more towards the belief that the more important the topic, the more empowered anyone is to express an opinion. There are vital topics in which many feel experts, for example, when we refer to related topics such as

THE CRITERIA OF THE SHEEP

health, finances, immigration, or couples, to name a few, anyone feels qualified to give an opinion. It is common today that if someone suffers from a disease, such as the one in the example, many have the right recipe to cure it; If your intention is to start a business to generate more money, you will meet individuals who have never started a business but who will try to explain the negative aspects to you, which is why starting it would be a bad idea; if the topic is immigration, you don't need to go to a lawyer anymore that everyone knows about it and can advise you on the matter; even those who have never been married feel empowered to have a say in matters of marriage. When it comes to an important issue in your life, always try to seek the opinion and advice of those who are truly qualified to do so. If it is about health, consult a doctor. If it is about finances, consult those who really have experience in the matter. If it is about any legal aspect, consult a lawyer, and you will see that it will be much easier for you to achieve your goals this way.

THE EMPATY

Another area where black and white sheep do not share the same criteria is when applying empathy. To explain this point, let's start by defining what the term empathy means. According to Wikipedia, empathy is the ability to perceive, share and feel (in a common context) what another being can feel. By understanding the concept, it is much easier to understand why the two groups we are studying have different attitudes towards empathy; On the one hand, we have that white sheep are extremely empathetic with other white sheep when they let them know that they feel bad for being going through a situation that they have in common. However, on the other hand, they identify you as negative; I mean that if a white sheep approaches another to tell them how sad they are for any reason, they will immediately receive a few words of relief, a pat on the back, and even a hug, depending on how you rate the seriousness of the matter; As long as the context is negative, you will find words of relief coming from the other white sheep or, at least, what they consider appropriate words in such a situation. They usually say something like: "don't worry, everything will pass" or "after the storm comes calm, hold on"; which translates as: "you don't have to do anything, just sit down, wait and see how everything improves or returns to normal in the future".

It can be said that white sheep, depending on the context of the situation, tend to discriminate when we refer to empathy. We already know that if it is a negative situation, they will react in the same way that they consider more appropriate, but what happens when the situation is positive if a black sheep approaches a white sheep and tells them how happy they are because they have finally reached their financial goals, the most common is that it is immediately This group is labeled arrogant as they fail to understand the criteria, context or ideals of a black sheep. It has surely happened to you that at some point, dominated by the black sheep that exists within you, you have wanted to do something out of the ordinary and have expressed it to others in your group, if this activity is something that goes outside the limited world Where the white sheep live, they will immediately have answered you with something like, "You are crazy," followed by a relentless array of reasons why you should get that idea out of your head.

If, on the other hand, you approach a black sheep to comment on the negative situation that is happening, it is most likely that it will respond with a comforting phrase such as: "What a shame you are going through this," followed by a group of words directed to reenforce while paying their attention to the solution such as: "and now, what do you plan to do about it?", this is due to the fact that the black sheep is clear that the problems are situations that we are obliged to face instead of ignoring them, and that our focus, rather than on the problem, has to be directed towards the solution; Now, if on the other hand, the referred situation is something positive, without a doubt they will

THE CRITERIA OF THE SHEEP

congratulate the one who achieved such merits since the black sheep understand the importance of achieving your goals.

As a black sheep, you will, at some point in your life, end up becoming a leader. Therefore, the ability to recognize, understand and share the feelings of others is a key skill that you need to develop if you want to have positive impacts on those who follow it. Being in harmony with the perspectives and needs of your investors or shareholders, your employees, and your customers will definitely strengthen your business. When we talk about your business, empathy will help you develop the ability to connect with those around you, contribute to your personal development, and open many doors on your long journey. In the modern world and thanks to the Internet, people are losing more and more the ability to communicate and empathize with others. For this reason, this will become a skill that very few will have in the future. Consequently, it will be an increasingly valuable tool.

SAVING IS NOT SALVATION

Another issue that is handled completely differently between the two societies is that which refers to where to place money. Most of the white sheep do not understand the difference between saving money and investing it. These are two completely different financial strategies; It is vital that as black sheep they are clear about these two concepts, white sheep are generally inclined to save as much money as possible, convinced that this is the best way to ensure their future because they believe that money is scarce they tend to save it in bank accounts with the intention of not touching it, without realizing that over time, that money is losing purchasing value since normally the passive interest rate of banks (the one that they pay savers for their money) It is below the level of inflation, which results in the value of money decreases over time. There are innumerable individuals around the world who, being millionaires, have lost their wealth slowly or in an accelerated manner due, in each case, to a high inflationary index or a drastic devaluation of the currency.

But keeping an optimistic attitude, suppose that none of these factors got out of control. Anyway, without realizing it, your money will be losing purchasing power over time as a result of inflation. On the other hand, the black sheep understand that money is to make more money and, therefore, they tend to invest in order to increase their wealth. However, it is okay to save some money for a specific reason, such as an emergency fund, but the rest of your money has to be working in one way or another, intending to make more money for you. Saving money in the bank makes the white sheep feel that their money is not their responsibility but the responsibility of the banking entity from that moment on. This attitude corresponds to their nature.

In this society, the belief that investing constitutes a high-risk activity has been strengthened. Therefore, it is better not to risk undertaking this type of activity because most cannot recognize the difference between betting and investing. In their world, they believe that they are similar acts. However, investment always has some type of risk. There are many ways to reduce it to the point where the balance tips in your favor; the gambler generally does not have any preparation and tends to risk his money, hoping that things will turn out in his favor. Instead, the investor prepares, studies, plans, and does everything necessary to ensure that the possibilities are in their favor. The better tends to seek short-term profits. In contrast, the investor understands that the best and safest returns generally occur in the long term.

Now that you know the difference, you can surely understand that saving is fine as long as it is for specific objectives set in the short term, but to achieve your financial goals, the best thing you can do is invest for the long term, thereby protecting your money against one of the greatest dangers always latent, which is

THE CRITERIA OF THE SHEEP

represented by yourself, and that is that by having easy access to your money you can fall into expenses as a result of unnecessary temptations. The environment in which we live is full of objects that we can classify as liabilities. That increasingly tries to make us see them more attractive to fall into the trap and spend money on things that have nothing to do with our objectives in life. Therefore, it is important that you take the necessary steps to protect your money from all the threats that exist today, including yourself.

VICTIMS OR VICTIMARIES

One of the most common problems faced by white sheep is that, according to them, the fact that they have not achieved success is due to the fact that they are victims of external situations over which they have no control, being victims of something or someone has become or in one of the most popular excuses in this society, they are convinced that they are victims of the government, the wealthy, their bosses, the climate, the things that surround them, age, the educational system, these among many other perpetrators, who have prevented them from arising, in one way or another these elements or situations have conspired against them in order to sabotage any attempt or opportunity that they have to advance or arise in their lives.

In this society, the impression has been created that everyone is the victim in one way or another of some kind of conspiracy, which is exposed every day and in which we are all suspects; In these times when the news travels faster and faster and has the power to reach a much greater number of individuals than it could reach in the past, you must be more careful than ever since, if you allow it, it will affect positively or negatively their gaze on different subjects; fake news seems to get popularity every day to the point that the presentation in these news media of different conspiracy theories has become extremely common. In this case, the question would be: What factors make someone a believer in these theories? Many studies have been done in recent years on this subject.

Most seem to agree that the educational level of each individual influences their decision to become a believer or not of a certain hypothesis, the white sheep, for the most part, dominated by their ignorance and fear of assuming responsibilities end up being faithful believers of these theories since they provide them the justification of why they are in the situation they are in; black sheep seem to be less vulnerable to this situation, this is possibly due to their tendency to educate themselves continuously and to have more information, which allows them to make better decisions as they are based on a clearer vision. Furthermore, this group is convinced that if something in their lives does not work out in the desired way, the only ones to blame and responsible are themselves for not taking the necessary measures to achieve these objectives.

Having a victim mentality goes far beyond the experience suffered. Even if it is true that at some point in your life you were the victim of some situation, it is important that you accept the fact as something that had happened, that it belongs to the past, and continue to get on with your life; will not solve anything by playing the role of victim, the only thing you will get is to attract the attention of some. They will most likely feel sorry for you. If you intend to victimize yourself to avoid your responsibilities, the only thing you will do is deceive yourself.

The white sheep that suffer from the victim mentality end up being convinced that their lives are not under their control and that there is also an entity out there deliberately wanting to harm them. In addition, they tend to identify themselves as victims of the negative actions of others. In short, those with the 'victim mentality' tend to blame other people and circumstances for their unhappiness or bad situation.

THE CRITERIA OF THE SHEEP

Certainly, those who suffer from this evil are victims, but they cannot see that they are their own victimizers because all this is generated in their minds and, as a consequence, becomes their reality, filling them with negative emotions, leading them to feel sorry for others and even themselves, thus develop a defensive attitude, expecting and anticipating for failure without assuming responsibility of any kind and without looking for solutions to improve your situation by letting your life be dominated by negative aspects such as frustration or fear, among many others.

THE FEAR

Many consider that fear is the most powerful emotion that any being experiences since its presence awakens survival instinct. Fear is a feeling generally caused by danger or perceived threat and causes changes in the individual's behavior, not only in their mental functions but also in their organic ones; the most common reactions are: confront the danger or avoid the threat; no sheep, regardless of its criteria, is exempt from living a life without problems or sometimes feeling fear in certain situations; where the two societies differ enormously is in how they cope with these situations.

In the society of white sheep, faced with a dangerous situation, they tend to avoid the threat; on the contrary, the black sheep, when presented with a dangerous situation or that causes fear, he usually faces this situation, confronting his fears is something that he is obliged to do if he intends to advance in life. This feeling of fear was developed in primitive times where we had to face predators, other kinds of animals, or existing dangers that threatened our lives. At present, other reasons have led to the development of many more irrational ones that produce in white sheep wanting to flee or hide from such events. Among some of the most common fears that exists today is the fear of failure, white sheep that suffer from this evil, sometimes consciously, others, unconsciously ignore, hide or eliminate their own efforts to avoid disappointment or failure, keep in mind that most of these fears apply to all aspects of your life and often do not allow us to balance financial success and other areas of our lives which will not allow us to be happy.

Another of the most popular fears that affect white sheep is the fear of criticism. As we already mentioned, in a white sheep society, everyone feels like an expert. Therefore, they have no problem expressing their opinion or criticism. When these are activities that others are developing; As a consequence, these individuals stop doing what they have to do, or they stop living their lives as usual.

They have pre dreamed it out of fear of what they will think or say about them in this society. They are also very common: fear of public speaking, fear of change, fear of disappointment, among many others that currently exist. Fear is a paralyzing feeling that does not allow the person suffering from it even to try to achieve their goals in the society of white sheep. Most assume that success is impossible since they have never experienced it by themselves, fear causes indecision, and, as a consequence, sometimes we act and convince ourselves that what we want is wrong or simply, for whatever reason, is unattainable. We begin to believe that what we want is not for us or cannot achieve it. All this makes fear one of the most common reasons to resist or avoid change as it prevents taking any action.

Now, the good news: overcoming fear is a skill that anyone can learn. You must be very clear that your fears are only causing problems and delays in your life. It is of the utmost importance that instead of walking away, ignore or avoid your fears start to face them. One of the best ways to do this is to start associating your fears with positive results instead of negative results without any foundation. This way, you are not ignoring or eliminating fear. You are simply suppressing your connection with aspects of negativity. Although it is true that the absence of

THE CRITERIA OF THE SHEEP

fear does not guarantee your success, you can be sure that if you do not learn to face them, you will not be able to achieve success since they will have a deadly effect on you that will not allow you to advance in your life. If you really want to achieve your goals in life, you are obliged to overcome your fears, start by having more confidence in yourself, have full conviction that you have the necessary capacity to make decisions and execute actions. All fears can always be overcome. When you have confidence in yourself and your purposes, you can easily overcome all your fears by being clear about what you want and taking massive action.

> "The number of ways you can live in one life is limitless. So why limit yourself? The sky is not the limit. Beyond the universe is."
>
> **Suzy Kassem**

CHAPTER 5

MAXIMIZE YOURSELF TO THE MAXIMUM

KNOWLEDGE HAS NO LIMITS
Knowledge is something to which you cannot set limits. It is impossible to know everything and, therefore, there is always something to learn. In its development, as a black sheep, you need to have this aspect extremely clear. The day you mistakenly start assuming that you know them all, many doors that could lead you to new opportunities will be closed, so it is important that you do not limit yourself, we live in a world of information and everything we want to know now, more than ever, is at our fingertips.

Although there are those who maintain that knowledge is power, I have never fully agreed with this idea, since if it is true that itis fundamental in their personal development as well as in their development as a business person, this constitutes only a potential power inasmuch as to get something done, it definitely has to be accompanied by action. Knowledge is the foundation that has made available to us the advances that have been achieved so far in the different areas of knowledge. It has

THE CRITERIA OF THE SHEEP

allowed us to be more capable, wiser, and it has definitely made us superior beings on our planet. If you are willing to purchase an addiction in your life, immediately assume that you are addicted to knowledge and that addiction will be permanent since you will never be satisfied. Knowledge is the most powerful weapon when going out to fight your own battles in life.

The simple fact of knowing how to apply their knowledge correctly can constitute the significant difference between success and failure. Knowledge simply refers to the condition of knowing something, which sounds very simple. But the reality is that it is constituted by an infinite universe of information that can only be acquired through education and experience. Knowledge is one of the main factors that will clearly place you in the group of sheep to which you belong. It represents the lens that will allow you to distinguish the good from the bad and to have the power to decide which is the best path to take. It will provide you objectivity when judging situations. The scope and power that knowledge can provide are limitless and will indeed allow you to achieve your goals in any area of your life.

Always keep in mind that success is not for the smartest but for the best prepared, and there is no other way to prepare than by acquiring knowledge. Believe it or not, most do not understand the importance of the positive impact of having the necessary knowledge on their lives. The simple fact that you understand that importance already represents a great advantage over other people.

Knowledge is no longer, as it was in another time, limited to a classroom, to what a teacher dictates, or what is written in books. In the modern world, there are many options and different ways of learning something new. We have access to knowledge environments, seminars, talks, conferences, etc. This gives us the option of taking them in person or simply from the comfort of our homes, in virtual form, through our computers; We are no longer obliged to read a book. We now have the option of listening to it through the Internet, among many other methods that have emerged today. We can have access to any type of information that we are interested in acquiring. Therefore, if you want to be successful, equip yourself with the knowledge that will prepare you. Thus, having the necessary wisdom to take the measures or actions that will lead to success in any area of your life.

SALES
In today's world and especially in the white sheep society, two of the fundamental skills both for our personal growth and for our financial growth have been undervalued, to the point that they do not seem to be necessary at all, I laugh. I am fierce about the skills of selling and the art of negotiating; whether we like it or not, we are all sellers, we are all buyers; that is, we could say that all, at some point, are negotiators regardless of the field in which we operate.

However, not everyone likes to act as a seller, probably because the idea that the seller is the annoying one behind you trying to get your money or the fear of being rejected is handled by who tries to sell. But for us, as black sheep and considering the undeniable relevance that sales have in the many areas of our life, it is mandatory to accept its importance and give this practice the priority it deserves. Consequently, it is necessary to begin to know the techniques associated with such practice.

Although many techniques have been formulated in the sales area, there are no written laws about how these should be applied. So when we refer to sales, you will have the freedom to apply the techniques you consider necessary for the case or use those you feel most comfortable with. When you practice the art of selling, I guarantee that in each of the situations that you face as a salesperson, you will have the certain possibility of learning

THE CRITERIA OF THE SHEEP

something new; By being more specific, you can always pioneer new techniques, develop new skills, or simply improve existing ones.

Sales and negotiations are available skills that can be achieved and developed through practice, which is to say that they are not unique and exclusive to the smartest or the most successful. They are available to anyone who simply has the desire to develop and train in the area. The mere fact of developing the ability to sell will open most of the paths that will lead you to improve financially. In this case, it does not matter if you work for a person, a corporation, or you own your business, always keep in mind that when you work, there are no limits in the sales area, you will not meet a boss who demands you not to sell so much, and if this is the case, this is definitely not the place where you want or should be, regardless of whether you are taking the first steps as an entrepreneur or your business is in full growth. Sales will be an essential part of your financial development. As a company owner, you will always be involved in sales and negotiation, willingly or not, in the sales area.

Sales, by nature, do not have an evil character. In fact, cataloging them as bad or good depends more on your criteria than on anything else. Let's understand that we spend a lot of our time selling, consciously or unconsciously, and I do not mean to sell material objects. I'm talking about selling ideas. When we have a conversation with our daughter about the time she should arrive home, what is happening? We are, without realizing it, in a negotiation in which she is selling you the idea of arriving at a certain time and you the idea of arriving earlier is selling; that is, everyone is selling. The same happens when she tries to reach an agreement about where to go on vacation: she wants to go to the beach, and you want to go to the mountains. In both situations, there is only one option: sell or be sold. So I recommend that if she wants to have an advantage in this type of situation, she learns as soon as possible to sell her ideas.

On the other hand, and continuing on the topic of selling ideas, who has not had the million-dollar idea at some point in their life? But those who truly achieve success with this or any other idea are those who not only execute but are also able to sell such an idea to others. For this reason, we see such productive businesses where the presentation plays a more important role than even the product offered. If you do not believe that it is true, ask yourself how it is that McDonald's sells so many hamburgers that they are not the best or the healthiest on the market, or how is it that Coca Cola is on the list of the best- selling drinks worldwide when it is not the best or the healthiest. These are just two examples among many that we could take to confirm that selling an idea is a fundamental activity in your company's success.

NEGOTIATION

As a black sheep, you will have an obligation to continually improve the art of negotiation since it is a practice that will be part of your daily life and, specifically, in business matters, it will be a decisive factor in your success. When you decide to leave the herd, you face many challenges; everything starts with an idea. Materializing this idea in the real world is generally not easy. From that moment on, one of the skills that you will surely need is the ability to negotiate. As a black sheep that you are, you have, implicitly, the ability to negotiate, but this does not mean that you do not need to perfect said practice, it is actually determining that become a master in this art as this will obviously make it easier to achieve your financial goals because through negotiation you can reduce conflicts and improve relations between the negotiating parties.

To better understand the concept of negotiation, we must admit that it is part of the process that will allow the parties involved to reach an agreement. The sales process is divided into three parts that have to work in harmony to achieve the best results, so

THE CRITERIA OF THE SHEEP

it is necessary to know and understand their characteristics, differences, and handling. These parts are: first, the sale; second, negotiation, and third, closing. The sale is the stage of the process where you have to convince the other party that a product, service, or idea is the best option for them and that you represent the opportunity to acquire or apply what is being sold; once the other party is in accordance with what was presented in the sale stage, a new process known as negotiation begins, in which the parties try to reach an agreement regarding the terms of said sale; Once some type of agreement has been concluded, you must go to the final stage of the process which we will call the closing, which is nothing more than the execution or materialization of the agreements reached in the previous stages.

By understanding the difference between these three points, we will achieve better results since we will be more efficient in each of the stages. We will be able to recognize when the sales stage is finished. This means to stop selling and start negotiating the terms. Once we arrive at the agreement at this stage, we will have to specify what was agreed, that is, the closing, which means consummating or ending the process. This practice is not limited only and exclusively to the financial area. It is also part of the process of interacting with others in our day to day. To appreciate its applicability in various areas, we are going to analyze two cases belonging to different areas, the first in the financial area and the second in our daily life.

In the first case, referring to the financial area, suppose that we are part of a transaction related to real estate, specifically a house: in the first stage of the process, you must convince the buyer that your product is the best, exposing points as they could be that this is the perfect house for him because it is in the perfect neighborhood, near the perfect school, with the perfect finishes or any other reason that may be binding on the client's decision; Once this stage is completed, the negotiation process will begin, in which the terms will be discussed and an attempt will be made to reach an agreement in this regard; Even though most think that the only and most important aspect to negotiate is reflected in the price, you, as a black sheep and good negotiator that you are, must be clear that there are other important aspects related to the price which can be negotiable, such as partial payments, or that other things such as furniture or the closing date of the negotiation are included in the price, among many other points. The fact that the client agrees with the terms proposed by you, and you, in turn, accept the proposals that he makes, that is, that there is an agreement in the proposals of both parties, constitutes the closure of the process.

Now, if it were the case to apply this practice to our daily lives, imagine a conversation with your partner in which you try to sell her the idea of going out to eat meat in a restaurant when she rather wants to stay at home unless dinner be it in a Mexican food restaurant; the simple fact of wanting to please her partner may lead you to give in to her position and consider or even agree to stay home, but in this case, she agreed to go out to eat, that is, you have already made the sale; Once this stage is finished, the negotiation stage begins where you could propose something like: "well, if we are going to eat Mexican food the way you want, we could do it at ABC restaurant where I know they also serve good quality meat"; to reach an agreement, it only remains to close the deal and go and enjoy a nice evening with your partner at ABC restaurant where she will be happy to eat Mexican food, and you will feel good about having the option of eating a good cut of meat.

Being a good negotiator does not mean that things always have to turn out in your favor. Many times, you must focus your attention on reaching an agreement that benefits both parties. One of the determining factors to become a master in sales negotiations and closings is in their ability to communicate. Being a good communicator is a key piece in this process. For

THE CRITERIA OF THE SHEEP

this reason, I consider it important that we talk about this matter in the next part.

COMMUNICATION

Communication consists of three elements or phases: the emission of the message, the message itself, and the reception of that message. To this last phase, it must be added that it is necessary that the message can be interpreted, that is, understood; If this characteristic is not present, the communication process is not carried out. This is due to the absence of a fundamental factor in the communication process that could perhaps be the most important and related to understanding. We mean knowing how to listen. Knowing how to listen gives us the ability to receive and accurately interpret the messages that are transmitted in the communication process. It is not possible to understand if we do not know how to listen. If we do not cultivate that capacity, the messages received will be misunderstood. Consequently, the communication will not be effective.

Therefore, the development of skills, including listening, in terms of communication, is decisive in all aspects of your life. This is a faculty that must be in permanent development. It is never too late to start cultivating your skills as a communicator. This will allow you to speak appropriately with all types of people. As you progress both in the financial area and your personal life, you will have to improve and increase your resources as a communicator simultaneously. Therefore, you will have to work on your ability to speak (communicate) better, listen better and ask the right questions, among other aspects. The way people communicate has a significant impact on the development of their lives. The importance of this skill is so great that in the case of black sheep, it can determine if it will eventually be successful or unsuccessful. It will be in the attempt. In the field of communications, the great power of conversations is often underestimated. Although it is one of the most basic forms of communication that exists, it is not the only one. A large part of communication is non-verbal. Body language is also It is a very important factor in the communication process. For this reason, it is that learning and mastering body language is essential to obtain better results when trying to communicate something.

As you progress on your path to success, the role played by communication skills increases, the ability to speak, listen and ask is an essential part of your growth, as in any other skill, if you want to get as close to perfecting it, you must to practice it continuously. One of the common factors that all leaders have, regardless of what area they work in, lies in the great ability they have to communicate effectively with others. For communication to be more effective, it is recommended to try to make some personal connection with your audience in order to create some kind of empathy, trust and make the individual or those who communicate feel calmer. This will also allow you to shape your message in the best way to adapt it to those who are listening to you, thus increasing the possibilities of effective communication. Being clear that communication is the most common and important form of interaction with others, we are obliged to permanently improve this skill since it will be fundamental when we try to sell or share our ideas, be it with our family, friends, our staff, team members or clients and, in general, with anyone to whom we try to convey our message.

In addition, communications will allow us to influence an individual's belief, attitude, intention, behavior, or motivation. All this is what we know as persuasion. Luckily for all of us, persuasion, like any other skill, can be learned and improved through study and continuous practice. The key to how to persuade others is to discover what your true motivation is. Once we can identify the motivating factor or factors of the other party, we can use these elements to our advantage. Your ability to communicate, persuade, influence, negotiate, and

THE CRITERIA OF THE SHEEP

generally interact effectively with other individuals is what will allow you to become the successful being you want to be, as long as you stay focused on what you want to achieve.

FOCUS

Another of the fundamental factors to achieve success is focus. If we do not stay focused on our objectives, strategies, execution, and in general, oriented towards our goals, these will be negatively affected. To achieve this, it is mandatory to stay away from the distractions that exist in our environments, such as social networks, cell phones or video games, television, texts, calls, or telephone messages, to name a few of an innumerable list of distractions that always seem to be at hand. The focus is the one that allows us to develop all our power when it comes to learning, memorizing, reasoning, solving problems, and, of course, in the process of making decisions. In other words, focus is vital in the process of elaborating our thoughts.

Focus is another factor that all those who achieve and maintain success have in common. The common factor is a firm determination to achieve their goals. The simple fact of reducing the time they dedicate to activities that distract them has transformed automatically. Only in time that can be invested in activities that help them advance towards their objectives, this simple practice already gives them a great advantage in terms of their competence, spend less time on these types of unproductive activities and set yourself as a goal Eliminate those from your day today to be as efficient as possible with your limited time, thus achieving the full potential power of focus.

Success is not always based on working hard or working harder. In order to turn it, your gaze at all times has to be directed to be as effective and productive as possible, and for this to happen, focus plays a fundamental role in this process. In white sheep society, it is considered a super ability to be able to do multiple tasks at the same time, without realizing that if we do not focus on a specific task, we will be wasting our effort; Many in the attempt to become independent and seek to improve their lives, by taking that step that turns them into a black sheep, drag this ideology ignoring that with this practice the only thing they are successful is to be less effective and, consequently, to move away from the desired results.

You have to be clear that the skill does not lie in doing different tasks at the same time but, on the contrary, is being able to focus on a single task at the same time, give that task the best of you and avoid being distracted by other activities Because when you focus your attention and your mental power on a specific task, you are giving your brain time to think only of one goal when you focus the power of your mind on that goal, amazing things happen: we make the best decisions, we analyze better our possibilities and generate great ideas, for all this, it is of the utmost importance to focus your mind on the desired topics and keep your concern under control and keep away fro, constantly switching from one topic to another.

We have then that each task needs independent attention to achieve a successful performance if we do not manage to focus effectively. It is impossible to aspire to have effective thoughts. The performance of our time will depend on the choices we make day by day. Therefore, it is advisable to recognize and maintain a list of priorities to be able to filter the important activities and those that are not, and in this way, focus on what is binding when it comes to going after our goals. Without knowing the direction, we will take or identifying priorities, we can waste our time in empty activities daily. In this way, the days, weeks, months, and, many times, years begin to pass without us moving in the direction of success. Being distracted in destructive activities, I call them that because, willingly or not, that is exactly what they do. They destroy our future, and many times without realizing it, we fall into that game that has nothing to do with our plans and keeps us away from our end goals.

THE CRITERIA OF THE SHEEP

THE TRIDENT OF SUCCESS

Although everything begins with an idea, we will not achieve anything without materializing or taking this idea to the real world. For this reason, it is that at this point, I would like to talk about the best way that exists to make this happen. I personally call it "The triangle of success" and consists of the following: preparation, organization, execution. Preparation consists of educating oneself, looking for all the necessary information, and in this way having the essential knowledge to make decisions and thus to be able to advance on our path to success, always bearing in mind that success is not reserved for the most intelligent but for those who prepare better, which means that we all have the opportunity to achieve success. This group of people, who many consider being at very high levels, are not gods or higher beings. The only difference between them and those who see them from below is that, among other things, these individuals took the time to prepare and acquire better and greater knowledge in the area in which they operate.

Education will allow you to break chains and free yourself from all those baseless beliefs that exist in white sheep society. Knowledge is what will help you develop a unique perspective of everything that surrounds you. Education is which will allow you to clearly see everything that exists around you and, in this way, expand your success rate; Achieving success will depend largely on your knowledge, vision, and criteria of life, and the only way to develop and improve these three elements is through education.

This brings us to our second point of attack, the organization, which consists of creating a work plan, a map that shows us the path to follow to reach the goal we have set ourselves. Without this map, it will be very easy to get lost or lost. Deviate from our ultimate goal. Creating a work plan is essential to achieve success because it will allow us to stay focused on our priorities. Of course, this does not mean that this map cannot be modified or adapted as appropriate once we begin to advance towards our goals. Therefore, adapting the work plan to the different variables that arise will be essential to achieve the proposed goal.

And the third step, in my opinion, the most important, is related to execution since it is about taking action and taking massive actions. It is not about doing a little every day. If you want to accelerate the achievement of your goals, whatever they may be, you have to take massive action and do everything you can every minute, every hour, every day, every week, every month, and every year with the intention of reaching them all his objectives. Taking massive action on all tasks is the only way to accelerate financially fully or any other success. Another goal that you aim for, you will only find success when you consciously decide where and when your journey will begin; from that place and the moment, your actions will determine your future. Preparing does not mean reading an article or a book. You must have to take massive actions to inform yourself or educate yourself as much as you can. It is about reading all the articles you can, all the books you can, asking all the questions That he wants and can if he has the right people at his disposal, this among many other ways that exist to prepare; Get organized and create a work plan and immediately take massive actions in all the points included in this plan, keep in mind that achieving success is no longer a secret to anyone, so making your dream come true will depend solely and exclusively on you. I have the full conviction that these three points are fundamental in the development of your life. Therefore, we are obliged to speak more extensively about each one of them.

THE CRITERIA OF THE SHEEP

> *"First of all, preparation is the key to success"*
> **Alexander Graham Bell**

CHAPTER 6
IT IS NECESSARY

PREPARE

Everything starts with an idea, but what really matters is the process that follows. Once you have the idea of what you want to do, the first step to follow should be to prepare yourself through education or acquisition of all the information you need. It can be obtained by referring or binding with that specific subject. This will help us strengthen our criteria and, in this way, build opinions, make decisions, and create our own point of view regarding the subject in question. Knowledge is invaluable, to the point that sometimes it is all that is needed to start your own business. Knowledge can provide you with opportunities beyond your capital or relationships. Most white sheep handle the concept that education or learning culminates in secondary school or, failing that, in university, which could not be further from the truth since learning is part of our personal development and, therefore, this process lasts all our life, every day we learn something new, and I do not mean just one thing, in fact, every day we are exposed to countless new information. It depends on you if you use it and assimilate it for your well-being or simply ignore it, thus closing the learning process.

Education is the fastest way to acquire knowledge. Although it is true that this can be achieved through experience, this process

THE CRITERIA OF THE SHEEP

can take years, and education is a means of speeding it up. Therefore, it is a fundamental piece on its road to success. It is a pity that many white sheep cannot recognize its importance.

Or are convinced that education is for a privileged group, which is far from the reality since the Internet gives them access to infinite information without distinction of race, religion, or economic position; Everyone, absolutely everyone has access to this type of information, and it will depend solely and exclusively on you to take advantage of this infinite source of knowledge, itis important for your financial development that you understand the potential power that comes from knowledge. Therefore, start to use all your resources to learn and collect as much information as possible. The simple act of unleashing your curiosity and feeding your appetite for knowledge will have a tremendous impact on your path to success, but the thought aside that financial success is for the smartest and in-store that this type of success is reserved for the best prepared, their desire to learn can be even much more powerful than the natural intelligence or abilities that other individuals may have, therefore, do not delay the matter and begin to accumulate as much information as possible from now on, be clear that the aged, gender or their current education, among other characteristics, do not constitute an obstacle when we refer to their ability to access knowledge.

Cultivating your education will infinitely increase your chances of achieving success. Financial education is the way to get your future in your hands since it is the only way to control how much income you will be able to obtain. The higher your financial education, the greater your possibilities of increasing your income. Always keep in mind that more important than simply learning something is learning something real and true. Therefore, make sure that your sources are the correct ones, be they people, books, experiences, or others. The informs. Misconception can be fatal when trying to achieve your success.

So, the best thing to do with your free time is to invest it in acquiring new ones with

Occupations, since you will improve your performance in this way, which will have a positive effect on your results; The more knowledge about a certain situation you have in your hands, the easier it will be to face any obstacle that may arise. In conclusion, there is one thing I can properly assure you, and that is that your chances of being successful in any area will drastically increase as your knowledge of that field increases; It will be difficult for you to compete with others in the financial area if you do not have the same resources that they have; in financial matters, you will always be competing and that the odds of winning the game are mostly in your favor will be based on your knowledge of the matter.

ORGANIZE

A business plan is an indispensable tool when developing your idea, whatever it may be. It represents a map that will show you the right way to the destination you want to reach. It is important that you establish a vision in your plan clear of growth and all the steps and actions necessary to achieve what you want. This plan constitutes the organizational structure of your idea. The essence of this map is to define and develop what is expected to be done, the purpose, the direction, and the steps to continue to advance in the project. It has to have specific objectives and goals. Originally a work plan is not perfect and in itself never manages to be. Therefore, changes must be reflected in it that allow you to adapt to different situations that are variable in the future. An updated business plan is vital for the real development of your ideas.

A good business plan will help you stay focused on your priorities, on all the specific actions necessary for your ideas to be successful, resulting in a more efficient process when it comes to achieving your goals. Share your strategy, actions, and

THE CRITERIA OF THE SHEEP

objectives with your work team so that all two are on the same page, be as objective as you can, and formulate your budgets as well as times in which such actions have to be carried out. When I refer to this issue, although I have named it that way earlier in this text, I do not like to call it a 'work plan,' since, in this way, I could be limiting it solely and exclusively to business when in truth the preparation, organization are the most effective way to carry out any idea regardless of the area in question; organizing ourselves will provide us with a clear vision of our future capacity. It is said, with certainty, that if one does not plan, the only plan will be to fail.

Planning doesn't have to be super complicated. By following this idea, you can simply represent it as a document that describes in detail what you want to do and how you plan to achieve it, no matter how complex or lengthy your execution plan is. I recommend that every day in the morning, before starting your day, evaluate all the objectives that you intend to achieve that day and analyze the different ways you can achieve them until you identify the one that seems to you to be the most convenient for you. The case. Evaluating your goals daily will keep you focused on your priorities, and by examining the possibilities of how you could do it, you are opening the door to new ideas with the intention of improving and little by little making your system as efficient as possible, planning is absolutely paramount in the process that will lead you to reach your goals, keep in mind that big things are made up of small things, therefore, dividing the big goals into small tasks that help you move towards your goal will definitely help and speed up the process. Fulfilling your mission, I can guarantee that once you discover the power of planning, it will become an essential part of all areas of your life.

In conclusion, there are many reasons why planning in advance in all aspects of your life is essential, through planning we will be more efficient and precise in our productivity, this without leaving aside its importance to stay focused on any moment and thus eliminate any distraction that wants to move us away from our main path, do not doubt that you will have to make adjustments in your action plan since there will be many variable factors to which you will have to face and adapt to overcome them in the best possible way. For all this, I recommend that you not only start planning your next moves in the financial area or in business matters but also start creating action plans for all the objectives that you intend to achieve, well either in the financial field or in the personal field, which at some point you can put together, thus creating an action plan for your life.

EXECUTE

Now let's talk about my favorite stage or phase. It is about "taking action," since, as I have said before, if it is true that everything begins with an idea, nothing happens until action is taken about it, even when you prepare or study when you try to collect information, you are taking action, when you organize or try to make an implementation plan, you are taking action, and that is the idea, take all steps needed to increase your chances of success. It is more common than you imagine to hear white sheep making comments like: "one day I'm going to have a lot of money, I'm already visualizing it," because I can guarantee you that visualization without action leads to nothing, inevitably you have to take massive action. If you intend to achieve your goals, you will find many others saying, "one day I will have a lot of money since I am sure that I am going to win the lottery," leaving everything to chance or luck without preparing or making an execution plan, of course, that can happen, but the chances are definitely not going to be in your favor. Although they take action and start, there is another group of people who never dare to leave this stage and begin to suffer from the so-called paralysis analysis. They continue studying, preparing, analyzing, collecting data without ever daring to create an action plan, much less dare to execute it.

THE CRITERIA OF THE SHEEP

I personally call them 'professional students' since this is the only thing they do. Studying ends up becoming their profession, analyzing, and continuing studying. They have great knowledge in everything related to theory, but for one reason or another, they never dare to take the step and lead this theory to practice. I hold the theory that taking massive action is more important than the thoughts themselves or, in many cases, over- anticipation, since action is the only way to move forward, to resolve situations, and to achieve the objectives that have been set, always be clear that everything begins with an idea or a thought that you can put on paper and study it all. You want, but if you stop at this step, I can guarantee that you will not achieve anything. If you do not decide to go out and take massive actions to make your idea come true, it will be challenging for this to happen. It is not about overthinking it. It is only a matter of taking that first step that will take you to your goal and start running as fast as you can to reach it as soon as possible. Success is waiting for you, and it only depends on you to achieve it.

Regardless of the goal you set out to achieve, it is of utmost importance that you take massive action as soon as possible and then continue to do so regularly. Moving forward is the most important thing, don't let the fear of making mistakes stop you at any time. Remember that mistakes are nothing more than learning opportunities on your journey. This is the time to stop thinking, stop reading and start taking massive actions. Thinking or meditating is important in the process, but it will only achieve results. Once you start to act, success itself has no owner or belongs to anyone. It is nothing more than a choice that you make yourself. Once you make such a decision, there is no other way but to take action. I am convinced that taking massive actions constantly is the most important ingredient to achieve success. It may be that the actions that we have to take are not the most fun or enjoyable option in which we want to invest our time. But if you want to be successful, this is the time when you have to put the playful child aside and start behaving like an adult, and in this way, start doing what you need to do to achieve your goals, even if it means getting out of your comfort zone.

By becoming a black sheep, you are no longer an average creature, which means going beyond the point where the rest of the herd would stop. It means doing much more than what others would do under the same conditions; Once you have selected your goal or goals, you have to turn achieving that goal into some kind of obsession in which you are morning, noon, and night, thinking and acting on it. We are talking about your future. Therefore, it has to be the last thing you think about before falling asleep. The first thing when you wake up, it is not about doing a thing only once, or when you have time, it is about making the time to make this happen. The best way to predict your future is by building it, and this will only be achieved through of taking massive actions.

PUBLICATE

The time has come to make decisions. In other words, decide if you want to do something important with your life. If the answer is negative, feel free to continue living in a world of the white sheep, to continue living in the shadows dominated by the fear of being criticized or, in his defect, for any other fear that does not let him advance. But if the answer is positive, it is time to let the world know your intentions, let everyone know that today is one of the most important days of your life since you have decided to take positive actions to make your dreams come true, whatever they may be. ; do not be afraid of being criticized and finish accepting that criticism will always be present since to be criticized it is enough that you are doing something, only those who do nothing and live in the shadows can be safe from them, like this start accepting criticism as perhaps some of it could help you in your career to success. You will possibly receive constructive criticism, but do not lose sight that these are the positive opinion only of a certain group. It is very possible

THE CRITERIA OF THE SHEEP

that you will also receive destructive criticism. You should pay the most attention to them since they can be the largest and best source of information to correct possible flaws in your project.

More common than you might think are cases in which customers are complaining over and over again, for example, about customer service. Company owners just ignore these complaints because perhaps for them, their company has efficient customer service. Then, when things do not start to go as planned, they seek the advice of so-called professionals in the matter. The surprising thing is that the professional, who charges a lot of money, generally diagnoses that the only existing evil in the company is, precisely, poor customer service. Company owners they fall into this type of situation very often. They tend to ignore the requests of their clients until a professional call validates such a situation. In my opinion, the most suitable professionals to diagnose this type of situation are made up of people or groups directly linked to the company, such as employees, investors, or clients. We are in the computer age where everything can happen at great speeds, take advantage of social networks, and let the world know that today is the day when you will radically begin to take the massive and positive actions necessary to achieve the changes that you propose, tell the world that you are no longer afraid of criticism and, on the contrary, that you are welcome. He is aware that the white sheep, without doing anything or doing very little, have become experts in criticism, a work that they take very seriously. They are always aware of the lives of others in order to express their opinions, be constructive or destructive, no matter the consequences, while black sheep are here to do something.

For this reason, they will inevitably be continually attacked by criticism from white sheep society, for this reason. It is of the utmost importance that instead of not expect criticism, which would be a very naive thought, you, as a black sheep that you are, are prepared for them. In this way, you can receive them, tolerate them, process them and, if necessary, take the necessary actions, as long as these generate positive results. Studies show that your chances of successor in your goals will increase about four times as much when you make a public statement of your goals and let everyone know your intentions and goals. I am not trying to say that it is something easy. At first, it can be very difficult. This is due to the lack of habit and the fears that we allow to dominate us in many circumstances, but I challenge you to try. In this way you can you can tell yourself that once you make your intentions public, you will feel a sense of satisfaction, tranquility and, with this, courage will be born, confidence will begin to grow, an indispensable ally when it comes to achieving your goals, it is time to start believing in yourself, the time has come to free the black sheep that exists within you and go out and fight for what you really want and that I do not doubt, that you really deserve.

POSITIVE

To win, you must choose to be a winner. Everything starts with a thought, and that thought undoubtedly has to be positive. There are those who think that incorporating this way of thinking into your lifestyle works like a magnet that will attract positive things to you. I mean that positive thinking helps us be clean from both mind and the environment, all the negative factors that surround us, and that many times do not allow us to see those beautiful and positive things that are in our way or within our reach. Once the decision to win has been made, the obstacles that come their way will not matter since their route is marked, their focus will not be directed to how difficult or big a certain obstacle is, since having proposed to win or finish the race, your focus and thoughts will be directed to how to overcome those things or situations that arise with the sole intention of slowing down or stopping your progress. Negativity is one of the oldest evils that has affected and continues to affect our society since it is highly contagious and highly addictive. Thoughts, whether positive or negative, work like magnifying glasses. If your thinking is

THE CRITERIA OF THE SHEEP

negative, it will be challenging for you to start the race since your mind will be directed to how difficult or almost impossible it will be to finish it. If that is the case and start, you will most likely stop at that point when you face the first obstacle since you will see it gigantic and impossible to overcome. Therefore, permanently incorporating positive thinking into your life is highly recommended. It is essential that you begin to visualize your actions. Many call this discipline meditation; it is not really important what you call it. Still, the important thing is the practice itself, take a moment every day and visualize yourself finishing the race, visualize how easy it will be to overcome any obstacle not only because of how small and insignificant that it is but because you have all the tools and the necessary capacity to overcome it. Visualize when the race ends and the feeling of satisfaction that you will enjoy in accomplishing this task.

To be successful in any aspect of your life, it is mandatory that positive thinking becomes a permanent practice or habit from now on. Black sheep are by nature positive, and due to this attitude, confidence. Although white sheep label them as dreamers and, many times, arrogant, this type of criticism is born by the simple fact of not understanding how positive thinking works. Whether positive or negative, your thoughts will determine your attitude in life, which will have a decisive impact on the results of the different tests or situations you face. To achieve financial success or in any aspect of your life, you have an obligation to eliminate the word failure from your personal dictionary since it is not an option. Keep in mind that your positive or negative attitude will be contagious and, therefore, you will be able to reach any of your circle of influence and, even, beyond, such as your partner, your children, your work staff, your potential, and current clients or, even, your investors, just to name a few; Without any doubt, by developing a positive attitude and approach, you will feel more confident and, therefore, you will have more control over the situation, this will help you make better decisions which will generate maximum performance. With a positive attitude, you will begin to radiate positive energies, which are contagious and will have a totally favorable impact on those who have contact with you. The members of your work team will perform more as they will feel better and more committed to their lives. Daily tasks, your clients will be more willing to purchase your products, you will generate more confidence in your investors. Therefore, they will feel more comfortable investing with you. Keep in mind that obstacles or difficult situations will always be present in our life. Therefore, it is essential that you understand that they are not there with the intention of stopping you on your way to success; they represent or are only an invitation to your growth and development on a personal level since once you have overcome them, you will become bigger and stronger as obstacles get smaller and easier to overcome.

THE CRITERIA OF THE SHEEP

> *"It always seems impossible until it's done."*
>
> **Nelson Mandela**

CHAPTER 7

MOTIVATION

MAKE MISTAKES YOUR FRIENDS
At this point, we will talk about perfectionism and how it can negatively affect your path to success. This is a common evil suffered by black sheep both at the beginning and in the development of their careers. By giving free rein and total control to the black sheep that exist within, you will become extremely competitive, which is why people often make the mistake of believing that excellence and perfection are the same thing. From now on, in all their activities, it is mandatory that they be excellent, which means going outside the standard parameters and giving, offering, or doing much more. This does not mean that their actions or the factors surrounding them have to be perfect to advance or do something. It would be naive to think this way since regardless of their work's excellence or actions, there will always be room for improvement. There is no perfect world, no perfect climate, no perfect person, or any other aspect of perfection that you are looking for. Do not make the mistake that many black sheep make that because they are waiting or looking for perfection. Although, as I said before, they end up doing nothing, do not be afraid of mistakes since they can become your friends. This depends on the way you treat or assimilate them. If you stop for fear of making a mistake, you will end up doing nothing. But if, on the contrary, you always act

THE CRITERIA OF THE SHEEP

with the premise that you have to proceed in the best possible way when the errors occur. Well, you have to accept them and learn through them how to solve, confront or avoid certain circumstances.

To understand a little more about this matter, let's analyze statistics of some of the most famous athletes in history: we have Michael Jordan, in his career he averaged 49.7 percent in field goals, this means that he missed more than half of the shots he took and yet for many he is considered the best player of all-time in the NBA. In baseball, we have Ty Cobb, who had a 367-batting average in his career, which means that he missed more than 6 times out of every 10 times he had to bat and, nevertheless, maintains a higher batting average than he has managed to keep any player in the history of the major leagues. We are talking about people who practiced their entire lives to achieve such feats, and as you can tell, they are nowhere near perfection, but they were definitely excellent in their respective areas. So, from now on, act with the awareness that mistakes will exist throughout your career. Both mistakes and problems are part of everyday life. Therefore, we have to accept and face them instead of ignoring them. We have to learn to assimilate the defeats as well as the mistakes. It is not about winning all the battles but about obtaining the victory in the most important ones to win the war. Always keep in mind that sometimes it is better to play the role of a fool in a certain situation or in a short time to be victorious in the long term. There is not enough money, the perfect partner, or any other aspect of life that is going to keep you from making mistakes or having problems.

It is best to take a deep breath in the face of any unexpected event and never let your emotions influence your actions or decisions in managing the situation. Although it is not easy at first, while you manage to control your emotions, it is better to take a moment not to make the common mistake of making decisions with a hot head of which many times we end up regretting. Take a deep breath, go for a walk. Use any technique that helps him calm down since only in this state will he be able to make the right decisions or at least act in the right way. Many of the most important knowledge that we obtain in our lives will be learned as a result of mistakes made in certain situations; Itis not by tripping over the same stone twice and learning through experience that you will gain the wisdom you need to face and make the right decisions when similar situations arise in the future.

BECOME AN ENEMY OF THE AVERAGE

We already understood that perfectionism is just an illusion that could negatively affect your performance, but there is something we must want to be all the time. It is to be excellent. From now on, you are obliged to give your best in every situation; While white sheep live in a world where conformity and routine prevail, you. As a good black sheep that you are. You will have to break these limitations. Your duty from now on is to get out of the ordinary by always giving your best effort to escape the area of the ordinary thus and enter the area of the extraordinary, which is the world where the black sheep thrive.

Let's look at it another way: if you are one of those who, having an assigned task, pick up your things at five in the afternoon and leaves work without giving that assignment the importance it deserves, don't let your ego trick you into thinking that you are the best employee in the company, or that you work harder than anyone else, or that you work a lot. You are nothing more than a white sheep with no intention of giving anything extra to help the cause in which you participate, something as simple as this can make the difference between the ordinary and the extraordinary, stay a few extra minutes, even when are not recognized in your salary, and finishing the assignment, that alone will not make you an extraordinary person. But you will see that in the long run, your efforts will be rewarded. Excellence is a habit that we can all develop, but it needs to be

THE CRITERIA OF THE SHEEP

changed or eliminated, that device that has been implanted in many heads that conditions us to think and act like white sheep. Unlike how many of those who manage to achieve success without being gifted think, they are beings like any other. The only thing that separates them from the herd is a vision. A way of thinking and acting differently from the ordinary, they develop different habits that anyone can develop, and among them is the habit of Excellence. These beings are obsessed with doing their best in many areas of their life or at least in certain areas, which certainly gives them a great advantage compared to those who settle for expected results. Many white sheep spend a lot of their time following others, be it on television, social media, or any other medium, always wondering how these individuals do everything they do without realizing that they are actually the same. Most of the time, the difference lies in the extra, by this I mean that while a white sheep lives in a world of the ordinary, the black sheep, adding the value we call extra, become extraordinary beings which, most Of the times it is translated as Excellence, it only depends on you to determine in what way you want to act in the world around you, in what world you want to develop, that decision is yours, start by understanding that it does not depend on any external circumstance such as age, sexuality, social status, color, gender, or any other excuse that you have put before you to justify being ordinary, and you finish understanding that being extraordinary is your own choice, which means that anyone can decide and develop the habit of Excellence, that is, that anyone can be extraordinary, begin to add that extra factor when interacting with other beings, when thinking, when saying, when acting in different circumstances, This is a critical step.

If you want to stop being a white sheep, leave the ordinary world, and become a black sheep still living in a world of the ordinary. Understand that your attitude and not the circumstances are what will make this happen. At first, it will surely not be easy because you will have to fight against ways of thinking and acting that have been planted in our brain and make us think and react in certain ways. Therefore, you need to feel comfortable with discomfort. You do not need to be excellent overnight in all areas of your life. Remember that we are trying to create a habit, and only through practice can we develop it. Start by selecting which area of your life needs more attention and focus on putting all your energy in that area to add that extra value that will lead you to be excellent in that sector.

THINK BIG, NOW BIGGER
For some reason, the white sheep are convinced that money is taboo and cannot be discussed, and many of them even see it as something evil. For this reason, the term greedy has acquired a negative meaning in this society. If I have to list five of the great differences between a white sheep and a black sheep, surely greed will be on this list. Greed does not mean anything other than wanting more, even if we link it to the issue of wealth or a monetary issue. I don't see where the problem lies in wanting more of something, because most people, in both societies, want to have more free time for themselves or enjoy with the people they love. They want to have more time to enjoy themselves. Different types of activities they want to have a healthier life, among many other desires. But the white sheep do see a problem when they want to have more money. At that specific point, the great difference between the two tendencies seems to exist, the good and the bad. Believe it or not, many white sheep do not even have in their most remote thoughts to make more money. I have heard comments like, "all I want is to have a simple life, a job that gives me enough money.

To pay my expenses", reasoning that I cannot understand since it seems that these individuals are convinced that a simple life has something to do with being poor. The other day I was at a meeting, and a friend approached me requesting advice on the subject of real estate. I gladly shared my knowledge of the area

THE CRITERIA OF THE SHEEP

with her. She was super excited since the sale of her property would produce the best for her. For her, it meant a considerable amount of money; what surprised me is that my friend's husband was sitting without even paying attention to the conversation, just as if he didn't care when the conversation ended and my friend left, I approached the husband and asked him

Igunté: Friend, don't you get excited knowing that they are going to receive an amount of money for the sale of the house, which is going to allow you to buy a better home?; Well, I must say that even today, the response I received from this individual surprises me: "No, Victor, in truth I am not interested in whether I live in that house or any other, I am not interested in whether we are going to earn money in the transaction if the next house is going to be more expensive or anything like that if I tell you the truth, I am someone who is satisfied with what I have, I do not aspire to more, what for? " That answer left me speechless for a few seconds. I thought: without aspirations, without expectations, what kind of individual goes around the world without wanting to have something else, without wanting to improve his life not only for him but for his family? I would dare to say that he even becomes a selfish person who only thinks about himself without even considering a benefit for his wife and children. These types of individuals are everywhere. It seems that they are already dead inside. They only go to work to meet hours. Without any expectations, it is as if they are just waiting to fulfill their time on this planet and nothing else. I cannot for a second imagine how empty the lives of these people must be.

In contrast, you will find that greed is one of the most common factors shared by black sheep, we always want more, we always want to be excellent at what we do, we are always willing to give something extra to try Being excellent in the area we set out to do, this feeling of wanting more and being better is a natural part of us. It is one of the reasons that drive us to behave in a certain way. By nature, we think big at all times, if the average is 5, our minimum goal, instantaneously, we put it in 10, but since we always think bigger, we propose to take that minimum to 20; this, I imagine, is what causes the illusion for many white sheep that black sheep are superior beings, which is nowhere near the reality since the only thing that separates them from them is how they assimilate the information and the way they act. Therefore, I extend an invitation to start thinking bigger and then bigger. If your goal is initially at 10, make it, thinking big, at 15, and then think bigger and find a way to achieve that at the same time as

20. This is a simple exercise that will create in you the habit of thinking in this way. There is nothing wrong with wanting more of something. We do not live in a world of scarcity. Therefore, start from this moment to think big. This is the only way to think if you want to go out into the world and achieve something else.

THE RIGHT SPEED

Another dilemma with which many are achieved refers to speed, I have heard phrases such as: "step by step", "little by little", "it is cooking", "life is a marathon, not a race "These are, among others, arguments and excuses that are used to justify not having met a goal; Referring specifically to the financial issue, this is not a marathon, it is a race that does not end, in which you have to participate at the maximum speed that we can, speed is linked to thinking big, in the financial world it is private the obligation to reach the goals as soon as possible to be able to start the next phase of the career, however, there are those who believe that this is not the case, they think that you do not have to go too fast, that making a lot of money stops in at some point, if that were the case, there would be no millionaires, just imagine that business person saying: "… I'm making a lot of money, I have to slow down", a totally absurd thought; if that works we should apply it in any area of life; Ask yourself: when do you want to be healthier, sometime in the future or now? When do you want

THE CRITERIA OF THE SHEEP

to be with the love of your life, with your family or with loved ones, at some point in the future or as fast as possible? Then why do we have to treat finances differently? The moment is now, not later, the time it takes to think about starting or attacking the next stage is time wasted and is irrecoverable, the pace of financial life is very fast, once covered one stage you have to tackle the next one immediately, remember you're in a race. The time it takes to move from one stage to another will obviously be reflected in the final result.

As expected, white sheep have any number of excuses to justify not moving forward in life. You have to learn to filter out those beings who give you advice all the time. It is very common that if you are talking to someone about an impediment they face to move forward, they will say something like: "don't worry so much," "go little by little." There is no bad intention in their advice, only that in your world, there is usually a justification or a reason why you cannot move forward, and because you cannot think of anything better, that is what it transmits to you. Don't be swayed by this kind of advice. You don't have to be rude to this individual; just listen to their reasons and keep looking for a way to overcome the obstacle you are facing, but don't put it off. The time is now. We are in an era where speed has become a very important factor in business matters, due to the great technological advance we have had in recent years it seems that there are more better-prepared individuals, therefore, always keep in mind that you do not He is the only one in the race, so moving faster and faster has to be one of his goals, he has to create a habit from this practice when it comes to reaching the client, he is obliged to be the fastest when it is about making a sale to a person, it should be faster if you don't do it like that and let your competition win all the races, rest assured that it will be very difficult or impossible for you to reach your financial goals. The client is not sitting waiting for you and is sure that if someone before you convince this client that he needs a product or service, he will proceed to acquire it even knowing that you offer the same but that for some reason. It never about being in continuous movement, be faster preparing and faster in planning so that in this way you can start executing faster, make this a culture, a habit, remember that every minute you let pass in reaching your financial goals is holding you back. Therefore, you have to sleep faster, eat faster, and exercise faster to get more effective results in the areas where you spend your time. From now on, you behave as if you are always behind already that not having reached where it has been financially proposed is interpreted as a delay.

TELL ME YOUR FRIENDS, AND I'LL TELL YOU WHO YOU ARE

This point is the only one that I literally transferred from my first book secrets in real estate many times. We fight to find this ideal, so the faster you understand and put it into practice, the faster you will feel and see the changes. When it comes to their personality, we are highly influenced, like it or not, by those closest to us. These individuals have the ability to affect our way of acting, thinking, our self-esteem, our mood, our decisions, among. In other respects, the power these people have over us is usually much greater than what we initially imagined. Let's stop to analyze this aspect. In the course of his life, he has made many changes. He has changed home, profession, values, ideals, partner, among others; we have in summary that at this point, practically all aspects of your life have been reassessed and updated, but most of the time, the updates do not include our friendships. It is possible that this statement may generate some reproach. But if you stop and think about it calmly, you will realize the importance of such an update little by little. Generally, our list of friends is made up of those with whom we have gone through many situations together, there is a story between us, either because we were friends from childhood or school, but think about it, the fact that your friend or A friend

THE CRITERIA OF THE SHEEP

consoled him when his girlfriend left him as a teenager. Does that mean he must share the same ideas all his life? Surely not.

Your friendships, like everything in your life, need an update. They should be reassessed from time to time to determine if they are still positively influencing your life. Your friends should inspire the best of you. We all transmit energy, so if it is shared a long time with beings who are negative, insecure, or destructive (white sheep), rest assured that you would be affected, regardless of your strength as an individual, you are not immune to a constant environment of negative energy or bad influence, if someone negatively influences you, it will end up affecting your relationship with other people in your environment, once you allow a negative force to infect your life and your spirit, a negative knock-on effect will occur that will not only affect you but also ultimately affect everyone around you, the values you live by should be aligned with those you spend time with if your friends are lazy, unhappy and negative, there is a high probability that he will end up adopting these behavior patterns. But, if you spend time with motivated, hard-working, happy, successful, and healthy people (black sheep), then you will be forced to elevate your game and bring those same aspects into your life if you want to have complete mastery of a positive environment in your life. It is important that he surrounds himself with those who inspire him to achieve greatness in his life. From this situation comes the proverb, "Tell me who your friends are, and I will tell you who you are," whether we like it or not, many times we end up converting or adapting to the environment that surrounds us, that is the reason why it is advisable to get together with beings that are superior to one in the areas that we want to develop, surrounding yourself with more successful people will be an accelerator in your aspiration to be the best possible in all the areas. Success attracts and generates more success. So it will end up being the direct result of your thoughts, those you spend time with, your preparation, and the actions you take. Why not select the best of the best in these areas? I mean, if you are constantly around wealthy people, you will learn that it is easy to earn money, but if, on the contrary, you spend most of your time around poor individuals, then you will constantly hear why it is so difficult to earn money. Surrounding yourself with the right individuals at this time in your life is essential as it will help you achieve your goals more quickly. You will feel totally stimulated as they will represent for you an inexhaustible source of inspiration and motivation, which will constantly be recharging its source of positive energy

THE CRITERIA OF THE SHEEP

"Life is like riding a bicycle. If you want to keep your balance, you have to keep moving forward"

THE CRITERIA OF THE SHEEP

Ray Kroc, age: 52, Colonel Harland Sanders, age: 62, or Wally Blume, age: 57, just to name a few. one of the most famous, because the lists of young people or of those who achieved great wealth at an advanced age are very long. Start to see the positive side of things, for no reason allow your negative thoughts to be in charge since these will only lead you to make excuses and, as a consequence, not to move forward, focus on ideals such as: "I am young!, I have all the energy and time to achieve it "or, on the other hand, direct your thoughts to aspects such as:" this is the perfect moment since I have the maturity and wisdom that I have acquired over time," is In other words, convince yourself that you are in the perfect age. Therefore, it is time for you to propose, prepare, organize and execute no matter where you are in life.

Now, you must be clear that although it is important to have a good idea, the process of executing it is even more important, as is the commitment that you acquire by start your project, the tolerance to accept your mistakes, and, many times, your failures, which could become an important part of your personal and business development, add to this your ability to evolve and adapt to possible changes existing in any market. All this, together with the passion you have for this or any project, is what will allow you to be ready to face and overcome any obstacle or challenge. Regardless of how old you are, always worry about improving your skills to communicate with people and your skills in sales, understand the benefits that working as a team will bring you, always have the door open to learning something, education must be continuous at any stage of your career. By developing these aspects, you will release the black sheep that exists within you. At that moment, you will realize that you are in the perfect age to pursue and achieve your dreams. Only by being clear about the factors that will lead you to achieve your goals will you understand since age is not one of them. This way, you can focus on the right areas that will allow you to function as a business person and achieve your financial goals.

CREATING YOUR LEGACY

Observing black sheep, trying to study their behavior to determine different types of patterns in their habits, I realized a trait that characterizes them. They always keep constructing their legacy as one of their priorities, which I found extremely interesting. More than to make money, part of the approach is: what to do with it. They worry about their future and that of their loved ones. Also, in this study, I came across two exciting groups: those who are convinced that they belong to the group of black sheep. I particularly think that this is just an illusion. I mean in the first instance many young people who have had financial success from one way or another and they have managed to make great fortunes that they use to live the present moment without considering the future, in a certain way they understand the importance of money since we live in a capitalist world where everything unfolds around it, and in keeping with that premise, they make more and more money just intending to spend it, they think that this is the only reason to make money. In this group, we find many of the young athletes who make their fortune once the professional teams sign them.

In many cases, paradoxically, they end up being poor. One of the reasons this happens is that by not projecting their gaze to the future, they do not worry about educating themselves financially and squander the fortune they manage to make in their youth. They only live for the moment. Therefore, no matter how much money they come to have cannot be classified as black sheep even if they have the illusion that while they manage this fortune, they belong to this group.

Although they are cautious not to lose their wealth, the true black sheep are not afraid that, for some reason, this will happen since they know and have learned over time how to make and

THE CRITERIA OF THE SHEEP

how to reproduce money. This is one of the characteristics that differentiate them from this group that we have just analyzed. The second group that I managed to identify is made up of individuals who, due to having money or some type of privileged situation with respect to others, live the illusion that this automatically turns them into black sheep, which is not, since, in reality, they do not know how to make money, most of them only live on the achievements or legacy created by their predecessors who were definitely or are black sheep, but the point is that this characteristic is not inherited. Belonging to this select group is something that one achieves by oneself. Therefore, it does not matter if those who preceded you did not have money since you definitely, can achieve it. In the same way, it does not matter if your predecessors have or have left you some kind of fortune and you have become an administrator of it. Understand that this is a legacy product of someone else's work, and the fact of being the administrator does not confer on him the title of black sheep. He is simply a white sheep that enjoys privileges derived from the fortune of another. It is not the same to manage what he built or the legacy left by his predecessor.

For example, my father left this, and I have made it grow to become this other, only at that moment is when you could begin to consider yourself a black sheep, that is, when you begin to behave not only as an administrator or manager, but that additionally brings its own triumphs in financial matters. To be the guardian or preserve the fortune or family legacy is not enough to have this title. Therefore, it does not matter if your relatives or ancestors left some kind of legacy, or if they have left fortunes. It does not matter if you have managed to make a lot of money during your youth by some fortuitous event or product of your talent. What really matters is that you educate yourself financially and learn to make money or maintain it and reproduce it. Only at this moment can you begin to add personal achievements in financial matters, which are the foundation of your legacy for future generations.

BE THE MOST INTERESTING PERSON IN THE WORLD

Starting from the idea that we are in negotiation at all times, in any conversation, we are selling something or selling something, be it a simple idea or a complex product (especially in the financial area). If we assume this, what actually happens is that multiple sales are being made simultaneously, which, combined, represent the likelihood of increasing your chances of success whatever your goal; Among all these small sales that make up a negotiation, there is one that I consider possibly the most important of them all, but to make this sale possible it is crucial to be convinced that you are, without a doubt, the best option that could have been presented to. On the other hand, I mean exactly that the most important sale that you will always be making will be your image, your reputation, thus projecting the absolute benefit that means having the opportunity to do business with you, and I do not mean to be arrogant. I mean the simple fact of believing in yourself and, convinced of that truth, reflecting to others that you are the best of the best, that it would be ridiculous to consider another option other than yourself, forget about the competition since this does not exist, the only reality in any presentation must be to make it clear that you. Your idea, your service, your product, or whatever you are offering is, without a doubt, the best option, and the only way to achieve this begins with yourself. Only when you accept that it is the best option can you project this into any conversation.

Practice your tone, the speed with which you speak, speak with confidence, it is of utmost importance that you always have eye contact, do not be shy about highlighting your achievements, recording your conversations and listening to them helps to identify points that influenced the development of the presentation. If you are just starting out in a certain area, focus

THE CRITERIA OF THE SHEEP

your presentation on potential success or potential profit, but if you already have experience in the field, focus on success in past experiences. It is crucial that whenever you are selling something where you have to include your image, do it casually. This can be achieved through a story or experiences from your past. I always have a couple of stories prepared to be presented in a negotiation dialogue since many times. These dialogues arise at unexpected moments. The purpose of these stories is to highlight your skills, qualities, achievements, in general, let the other party know a little about you, of course, always being humble and in a way casual, so you avoid looking arrogant; keep your posture and try as much as possible never to lose eye contact, this is extremely important as it makes the other party understand that you are paying attention to everything he says, do your best to keep a smile now that it represents a symbol of friendship, be, as far as possible, brief in your answers in order to give the other party space in the dialogue.

Initially, it is not about exposing or selling the product or service you offer, since, regardless of the excellence of your product, if you cannot sell your image and the other party trusts you, the possibilities of not making the sale or not finalizing the negotiation will be greater. Always keep in mind that feelings are contagious. By this, I mean that if you speak with passion about a certain topic, the other party will be able to capture this feeling and even share it, likewise. Suppose you make your presentation casually as much as possible. In that case, it is sure that the dialogue then does not generate any type of tension. Therefore, I recommend focusing the presentation on positive feelings such as passion and happiness, which could be expressed with a simple smile, always be casual. These, among others, will be factors that will help the negotiation outcome and increase your chances of reaching your goals. In short, try as much as possible to be yourself. Do not forget that you are the best option the other party can have because you are the most interesting person in the world.

TO INFINITY AND BEYOND

Once we break the false belief that we live in a scarce world and we begin to see and understand that it is the opposite, that we live in a world of abundance where there is an infinite number of possibilities and opportunities, especially in the financial area, by having This idea is clear, the question would be: how much do you want? and the only adequate answer to this question would be: "I want it all." Remember that we live in a world in which the majority belong to the group of white sheep who have the idea that the world is scarce, and for this reason, they have attributed a negative character to want to be ambitious. If we examine the meaning of this term, we find that ambition is called the desire to obtain power, wealth, or fame. There is no negative aspect in having power, wealth, or fame, this is something that black sheep are clear about, and it is the main reason why they always think big. I can assure you that what you consider great thoughts for your future today, they will become little thoughts tomorrow. If you still have doubts about it, take a look back at your life and remember how much you wanted to do or earn 10 years ago, 5 years ago, and compare those financial goals with your current goals, most likely is that they are not alike, this is because when you start if your goal is to achieve X amount of money, shortly after reaching it your next thought will be: and now how do I manage to make XX amount? I assure you that when you achieve this goal, you will begin to think about how to achieve XXX, so why not free yourself from this process and accelerate the achievement of your goals? I mean, why don't you decide, from the beginning, to consider the possibility of reaching XXX. Being clear that we live in a world of abundance, reaching such a goal will not be a problem, always being clear that everything is unprecedented until it happens for the first time, that nothing has ever happened until it happens

THE CRITERIA OF THE SHEEP

for the first time, just look around. We live in an age where there are more billionaires than ever before, and this list keeps growing every day. Therefore, I recommend that you extend both your thinking and your goals and make them bigger than initially projected. I mean that once you set a goal, multiply it by three, or by five, or, better yet, by ten, do your best to think big without putting limits on your imagination. In this way, you will speed up the process and expand your capacity, even far beyond what you can imagine, make big thinking a habit. Set yourself clearer goals and give way to creativity, do not let yourself be dominated by any kind of limit or fear, it is the only one way to release your potential which is unlimited. All of this will inevitably lead you to act, think, and do bigger things than even you thought possible, and inevitably thinking big will become a habit.

While it may be true that big goals are intimidating at first, I guarantee that once you get over this fear, you will start to see everything differently. Bigger goals or than initially seem crazy, they will become fuel for your motivation. They will become more enjoyable and satisfying. You have to visualize what the positive impact on your life will be once you achieve them. Thinking big will generate an absolutely positive change in your behavior. It will create in you a broader vision that will allow you to see things that you could not see before. In this way, you will experience a new way of thinking in which ideas will begin to flow. More clearly, this new stage will help strengthen one of the pillars of success that is motivation. Having big goals and imagining achieving them will cause you to feel motivated throughout your journey. That strength, motivation, It is a resource that we will never have in excess. The channeling of that energy is what will make us set our goals as reaching infinity. Beyond achieving, in this way, that thought, action, and results have the same intensity.

MASSIVE ACTIONS
Every day hundreds if not thousands of thoughts pass through our minds, some good, some bad, some small, some great, perhaps we select some to execute, and we go through a planning process, but sometimes some reason arises why we discard, or we postpone the action we should take to make this thought materialize, this happens more frequently than you might initially imagine. For this, we usually base ourselves on something that never seems to end: excuses, we blame external phenomena such as the weather, the economic situation, and, in some cases, we even blame third parties. If the black sheep are clear about something, it is that the only way to achieve their goals is by taking action, regardless of how much they plan. Understand that mistakes are part of the process. Therefore, as much as you plan, they are inevitable. Committing them from time to time does not mean that it is the end of the world and much less of your project. You must assimilate these mistakes and learn from such situations to avoid falling back into them in the future. So the more time you plan, the less time you will spend taking action, also know that. No matter what you do, the critic will always criticize, the haters will always hate, and the only way to avoid being criticized or hated is by doing nothing and thus going unnoticed, a situation in which you should not fall if you want to arise or achieve your goals, you always have to be alert not to fall into the game of these losers who only try to justify themselves in your world because they have not been able to achieve what you are trying, and the only weapon they have is to attack with destructive criticism those who are trying to do something. I can guarantee you that surely, they have already gone through this process before, I mean the process of feeling encouraged by an idea or project and immediately eliminating it for some excuse that arose while they were preparing to exercise his plan of action and, as an obvious consequence, nothing happened. Although it sounds straightforward, for some reason, it is a part of the process that many cannot overcome. I mean

THE CRITERIA OF THE SHEEP

simply trying to take action, but not any type of action, although the simple fact of doing it already means progress. You have to make sure that the actions are consistent with the thought, idea, or purpose. If you intend to achieve great goals, your actions must be massive to balance success tips in your favor.

We all have the capacity to act, and it is only up to us to take advantage of this gift. We do not need anything special, only the will and the true desire to move forward to take the necessary actions. The results that are obtained generally go hand in hand with the type of action that is taken. That is, if your actions are slight, you will generally obtain slight results, but if your actions are massive, the chances that the results will be much greater are inclined in your favor. If you really want some change in your life, you must take concrete actions. I repeat, I always refer to massive actions since many, even when breaking the first barrier that is to try, fall short in the type of actions they take and, therefore, they do not achieve the expected results. Many do not know the difference between being extremely busy or extremely productive. Productivity or generating income is a fundamental element to achieving your financial goals. You must always be alert in which activities you invest your time in order to focus it along with his energy to those that will truly bring him closer to his productive goals. Never forget that we live in a world of abundance where having more is available to everyone. We can have more money, happiness, security, or whatever else we want. We do not have to settle for what we have at the moment since by living in a world of abundance, we have access to more, and the secret to achieving all this is to take action. Therefore, if we want to have more, we have to take massive actions in order to achieve much more than what we are looking for.

"The will to win, the desire to succeed, the need to reach their full potential ... these are the keys that will open the door to personal excellence"

Confucius

CHAPTER 9
SYMPTOMATOLOGY

DREAMERS
Only by understanding that we live in a world full of abundance and without limits can we give ourselves the pleasure of dreaming and achieving whatever we want. The black sheep understand perfectly that nothing has been done until it is done for the first time, which means that the fact that it does not exist does not mean that it is impossible. They dare to dream of reaching the Moon, other planets, traveling the galaxy, create devices that allow us to communicate from anywhere, and at any time, they dream of flying. In general, they have in common setting goals that would be ridiculous or simply unreal for the vast majority. For this reason, they are usually attacked, even often by people close to them, with phrases like "stop dreaming" or "you have to be more realistic because most individuals do not understand that dreaming big is what will allow us to achieve great things.

I am going to clarify a point: I use the word or the term dream because I consider that it is the expression most commonly used by society to refer to something that they long for or desire, and although most see it only as such, as dreams, in truth only a few

THE CRITERIA OF THE SHEEP

of us manage to understand that they are not such a thing, they are really visualizations that the black sheep we use to be clear about where we want to go since we understand that if we do not know what our goal is, how we could then reach that point, it would be almost impossible, that is why we worry about visualizing in order to create a plan of work focused on reaching such a destination. Regardless of the area where you develop, visualization is a fundamental part of the process of reaching your goals. At first, it is not easy since once we have an idea, a dream, and we dare to visualize it. It is generally followed by a series of objections, excuses, or situations that get in the way of our purpose of reaching the goal set, and, consequently, the attempt to achieve something different in life dies at this stage. Do not allow these negative thoughts to destroy your possibilities. Although it is true that our goal may be difficult, it does not necessarily mean that it is impossible, and most of the time, all the problems or excuses we create are in our heads. It is normal to have you fear of the unknown. The difference in your future is in how you face these fears. If your position is that your goal is just a dream, it will remain on this plane as something unreal. The same happens if your position is to visualize but followed by a series of excuses that justify not trying. You have to do everything possible to eliminate all these negative reasons from the process. Although they can indeed be problems, they surely have solutions and, as a black sheep, you must understand what we already know, that problems are nothing else. What opportunities are presented to us to face these obstacles and solve them to achieve the success that we set out to do?

The secret or key to facing all these obstacles is a positive attitude. Once you manage to develop the habit of thinking positively, nothing will be seen as something impossible to do. The human brain works that way if when creating thought is followed by the idea that it cannot be done, the brain does not even bother to keep thinking about it and, therefore, discards the thought, but if on the contrary, we think that it can be done and that we can do so, our thought immediately changes and our intelligence is focused on looking for the different ways to achieve the proposed objective. Visualization is a valuable practice that will help us, among other things, to stay focused on our goals, we live in a world full of distractions, and we could easily deviate from our path pursuing something that catches our attention and that has nothing to do with our goals, for that when visualizing we have to focus on the things that are truly important, and that will bring us closer to the destination we want to reach. In addition, the visualization process will help develop your creativity and keep you stimulated in achieving your goal. Therefore, you have to dare to dream big, understanding that this is nothing more than visualizing your goals for the future.

YOU ARE DIFFERENT

In the society of white sheep, there is a pattern of behavior that dictates how they should act in all stages of their life, from childhood to old age. For example, how we should go to school, what behavior we should assume, how we are forced to get a job and try to keep it all our lives, among many other patterns. Any individual who has the audacity to break out of these behavior patterns is immediately branded as someone weird, different, as if this individual suffered from some kind of disease, these are the so-called black sheep, as if the very idea of being different was something bad, personally. I do not share this ideology. There is nothing wrong in being different, in breaking out of behavior patterns, as long as we are not violating the space or the rights of others. This is one of the tests more difficult than we have as black sheep, I mean that for no reason should we allow society to break our spirit or our way of thinking and make us behave like one of the flocks.

For a short time, I have known two young adolescent brothers that caught my attention, female and male, both great, with

THE CRITERIA OF THE SHEEP

immense potential, the girl tends to excellence and, therefore, tries to do everything she does, something excellent, which is why she is continually attacked by family and friends. I couldn't believe it when she heard advice from these people such as: "... you have to take it easier, you are too young to worry so much about things". We are what we do, and excellence is a habit that, although most of us have to create it with practice, there are a few privileged few who are born with this gift, develop they roll from an early age the habit of being excellent. There is nothing wrong with worrying about doing things the best possible; on the contrary. We should take them as an example to follow from my point of view. But because it is such an unusual habit, it is easier than society to treat this situation as if it were a problem rather than a virtue and try to break this behavior and bring these naturally genius individuals into the normal world.

On the other hand, there was the brother, another great young man with a genius not recognized by society. On the contrary, specialists already have a name for this type of behavior. Thus, when referring to this young man, he is classified as an individual that has a special situation, giving it a negative connotation for the simple fact of being different. Suppose the idea is put aside that the special condition of this individual does not lie in the fact that he does not follow the patterns of behavior of society. In that case, it could be seen that such a condition lies in having degrees of concentration that, for many, are impossible to achieve. He can easily understand and solve mathematical and physics problems that would be impossible to solve for the vast majority. Understand that being different is not a problem. The fact of not having excellent grades in school does not mean that you have poor intelligence. According to Howard Gardner, there are different types of intelligence that may not be common knowledge. When we meet special beings who can, for example, playing of musical instruments in an exceptional way without having studied music, we are in the presence of a person who possesses an unusual musical intelligence. Thus the footballer who has to make decisions in a matter of seconds about what to do with the ball or how to dodge his opponent or take a shot at goal, and all this is done naturally. We are definitely facing the case of a person with great bodily intelligence, but if they did not manage to have excellent grades in the educational system are most likely to be considered unintelligent people. Do not allow society to break your spirit since, many times, what makes you different can become your greatest virtue in the future if you want to have a good result. The middle class of society behaves like an average person in society, behaves like a white sheep, does not go out of the normal patterns, but if you want to achieve extraordinary results, you have to be different and behave like a black sheep.

HUNTER OF OPPORTUNITIES

It is interesting to see how problems are seen, analyzed, and faced in different ways in the two societies: on the one hand, we have the white sheep society where the word problem generally represents something negative, something big, and possibly very difficult. To solve and it is common for most of these people to avoid facing it, thinking about the complexity and consequences of it. On the other hand, black sheep understand that problems represent possibilities, the bigger the problem, the bigger the possibilities. The magnitude of the problem depends on the plane from which it is observed. White sheep usually see the problems from below.

For this reason, they seem very big and also feel that the problem is above them, while black sheep tend to see problems from above, which creates the impression that they are small and they feel above them. Consequently, they are not intimidated when facing them. Personally, I continuously work together with my team to try to eliminate the problem word from our vocabulary and replace it with a situation. In this way, we manage to remove the negative environment from any problem we are

THE CRITERIA OF THE SHEEP

facing. We were generally raised with the idea that a problem is something negative, but with the simple practice of substituting the word problem for the word situation, all negativity is put aside, which allows for an immediate positive approach in addition to being able to see it more objectively, which is always very important when deciding what actions to take.

In order to develop our maximum potential, it is mandatory that we stop seeing problems as an opposing force and instead understand that they are nothing more than situations that generate the opportunity to learn, improve, adapt, and evolve and, therefore so much, to grow personally, financially or in any area in which we are facing such situation; This way of thinking will help you to achieve success more easily since every time you face one of these situations you will have the opportunity to improve, adapting and, as a consequence, evolving, which will generate continuous positive changes in your life. Due to the negative environment that society gives to problems, it is easy to fall into this game and also react negatively to any situation that comes our way. For this reason, you always have to be alert and put your feelings aside to act accordingly. Objectively, only in this way can we take the most appropriate decisions and actions to face this situation. Let us understand and accept that problems are part of life, regardless of what area we operate in, they will always exist, but the difference can be made by you depending on how you see, analyze and react to them. If you start to see this situation as an opportunity to improve will be giving you the positive environment necessary to deal with them, which, as a consequence, will make you more skillful and more effective when acting in this situation. Thus, you become the one who solves problems, the essential foundation of the sheep black.

It is certainly true that all this can be a bit complicated. For this reason, I am going to give you a piece of information that has helped me in an extraordinary way to stay focused on how to face these situations. It is nothing more than the practice of changing the approach: I mean that instead of focusing on the problem, put all your attention on the solution. The problems are easy to identify, but sometimes, once identified, we fall into the game of dedicating our attention to questions that do not solve the problem, at least at the moment, such as: Who is the culprit? Why is this happening to me? The focus should be on how I solve the situation, which would allow us to direct our gaze towards the factors that influenced such a situation to arise. Therefore, when a problem arises, the immediate reaction should be to find the solution. With only the practice of changing the approach, I guarantee that it will be much easier to trivialize, confront and take the necessary measures to solve adverse situations.

LOVER OF CHANGES

Loving changes implies that by living in an environment or society full of rules and social parameters that do not make sense to us, we are in the continuous task of making or making positive changes to improve the situation, no matter how much at first, we deny ourselves, we have to understand that we are by nature black sheep and becoming one of them is a life decision. Many times, it only depends on releasing all those desires that we have repressed because they are not in accordance with the parameters of the society of the white sheep. You will only be able to evolve when you make this decision. At that moment, your life will change completely both in the personal field and in the work environment. Surely you will begin to pay attention to issues that you previously ignored, your way of seeing the problems will change since You will understand that these are possibilities, you will begin to develop new skills that you yourself did not imagine were within your reach, you will undoubtedly experience a transformation in your personality, and although it is true that at first, any change can generate fear, you have the obligation If you do not get carried away by this fear, you must make the decision and let it happen, I assure you

THE CRITERIA OF THE SHEEP

that once this happens, you will feel much better since by nature the black sheep are lovers of changes and this is the first of all they.

You will feel so good when this happens that you will want to share the well-being you experience with other individuals, and this will lead you to try to make changes to generate a positive social impact in current and future generations. By allowing your personal transformation, you will realize that you can achieve your dreams since these have always been a visualization of where you want to go. You will begin to develop your curiosity and direct it to problems that you think you can solve or situations that you are sure can be transformed so that others can enjoy these changes. This implies understanding that this process begins within oneself and not it depends on external situations. We will become proactive thinkers, which will lead us to be those who solve problems and promote positive changes. At this time, many situations that were previously accepted by the simple fact that society, in general, will be subject to evaluation and analysis in order to determine whether they are for or against our nature. Accepting change will be part of your growth as a person, and being able to adapt to changes will help you evolve and survive in the modern world, which will undoubtedly increase your chances of success. Personally, I prefer drastic changes and thus deal with all possible situations at once. It is like bathing in a pool of ice water, I disagree with first touching the water, then putting my foot, then a leg and so on ..., if the intention is to get in, I prefer to jump at once, but as in the end the important thing is that its mission is fulfilled if you prefer to touch it first, fine, but be aware that at some moment you will have to enter whether you want to or not, I mean that if you do not want to make the changes drastically, you can make small changes at the same time and thus move forward as you feel comfortable, the important thing is always to move forward, failing and making mistakes is part of a positive process of change, which in principle and naturally is understandable.

As an example, assuming that learning to walk implies a positive change. Let's observe any baby in that process, no matter how many times she falls or how hard she hits. She keeps trying until he achieves her goal. I mean that the search for positive change justifies mistakes, and that is how we will have to assume it from our beginnings. However, for some reason, society has condemned failing or being wrong in almost all its forms, if you are wrong in an exam in school, you are penalized; If you play baseball and fail to hit a pitch, you will most likely be judged, and if you do it three times in a row you will be penalized. In a soccer game, very little is said about the goalkeeper who stops a goal since the focus of attention is directed to criticism in case he fails. These are just some examples of why, over time, many people begin to be afraid of failing or making a mistake. Consequently, they prefer to avoid losing than to try to win. Let's turn our gaze to that baby and assume that positive change is possible; no matter how many times we fall or how hard we hit ourselves, we just have to get up and keep trying until it happens.

CHALLENGES ARE FASCINATING

By understanding that changes are inevitable and part of the process, you will begin to see them as challenges that you will find fascinating. If you are comfortable at this time, then you are in one of the worst places where you can be since most of those who come to feel this way fall into a state of satisfaction and lethargy that generally does not allow them to advance further. Therefore, it is of the utmost importance to be alert to this state, but if this happens, shake yourself off and keep moving forward because change is the secret of your personal development. You always have to be making changes. Whether you want it or not, the world is going to move forward with you or without you. Therefore, it is better that you adapt to the current changes, even more so in this modern world in which we live in which many

THE CRITERIA OF THE SHEEP

changes happen from one second to another. Those that are not able to adapt and evolve are doomed to extinction. The good news is that by letting the black sheep within you take control, the changes will no longer be a problem since the nature of black sheep is to love changes because they understand how important and fundamental, they result in their development not only at a financial level but at all levels, for this reason, when occurring in different areas, it will begin, among other aspects, to think differently, to see things differently and to speak differently. Consequently, one of the most important changes will also occur, very common in black sheep. I mean the change that has to do with the habits, which will be an essential part of their transformation in personal development in all areas.

Let's see, some of these changes will occur consciously and others unconsciously. However, the more positive habits you include, the faster the progress in your life will be. Therefore, you are obliged to start changing all those negative habits that you are used to and that stop or do not allow you to move towards positive habits that are the ones that let all the good flow. The topic of positive habits is vital and extremely extensive since there are many. However, I would like to name a few, which should be a priority so that your life flows in a better way in all aspects. It all starts with a thought or an idea. If in white sheep society that thought or that ideas are treated as dreams, for black sheep they become goals, therefore. At the same time, most have as a strategy the hope that one day something will happen, you, rather, start thinking about the different ways to achieve this, in the understanding that hope is not a strategy and that it only depends on you that said objectives are specified, in this stage is where all the possibilities are analyzed. An action plan is created that results in one of the most common habits among those who manage to be successful, and that is nothing more than directing their attention to fulfill their objectives, which leads us to the second habit that is none other than education or preparation. Therefore, they are always open to acquiring new knowledge and understand that the education process never ends.

Consequently, they are always educating themselves. According to statistics, those who achieve success read between 2 to 4 books a month while the rest read between 1 to 2 books a year. Obviously, this is not your case since if you have reached this point, this implies that you have no problem with reading or learning. You must be very careful at this stage because although education is indeed continuous, you have to know, even if you continue to educate yourself when to start practicing the third habit that is to take action, many in this process become what we already call 'professional students' and what do they do? Only to study and prepare without taking any type of action. Although the saying says that "knowledge is power," I do not share this criterion. I believe that knowledge is potential power since without taking action, nothing will happen. Therefore, it is mandatory that you take actions, start practicing another habit, which is to measure all your actions through the results obtained, this will allow you to apply the corresponding adjustments to improve those results, and you will also begin to value your time, which is the most valuable asset we have in life. Another common habit in successful people is that they focus their attention on their health, they begin to value mental or physical practices previously criticized or ignored such as meditation or exercise, they develop the habit of having a positive attitude towards any situation, they understand that making mistakes is part of the process. Therefore, they stop being afraid of being wrong. Starting to create daily routines will develop self- confidence, situations that are avoided by others will become challenges for you.

You will understand that feeling uncomfortable is a sign of progress. You will begin to control and manage your emotions in a more conscious way. Understanding that objective decisions

THE CRITERIA OF THE SHEEP

cannot be made when acting emotionally, so you have to start managing them more intelligently. Be more disciplined in all areas of your life while keeping in mind that perfection is the number one enemy of advancement. All this will help you progress faster, at a speed that some may not understand, and while you think that you were lucky in achieving your goals, you will have the certainty that luck and the achievement of your goals will always be on your side because it does not depend on external forces but on his own work which is the product of his good habits.

BRAVE

I believe that courage resides in us naturally. Due to a system based on fear or, better said, terror, we have stopped being brave for fear of making mistakes and, consequently, of being judged, among many other things. So I think we have to go back to our origins, by this I mean that in some cases we have to think as we did when we were children when we did not mind falling if the objective was to walk, we got up and we would try again until we succeeded. When if the goal was to ride a bicycle, it didn't matter how hard we hit ourselves when we fell; we simply got up and tried again. A baby, by nature, is born without fear. If not, let's take as an example the baby who, when seeing an insect, grabs it without any fear and, sometimes, even eats it, and if it tastes bad, he does not do it again. Only when he sees an adult screaming or with a gesture of fear at the insect does this baby begin to react in this way to the same situation. This is what I mean when I say that the nature of all of us is to be brave since we were born with that gift and that for different reasons, we sometimes end up losing it over the years. We have to go back to being that child who is not afraid of anyone, who saw an invincible superhero and wanted to be like him, who understood that pain is often part of the process to achieve their goals and that there is nothing wrong with being wrong, only then will we be able to develop fully and give freedom to the black sheep that we have inside so that it can think and act freely without fear of anything, which will allow it to advance in life and face as common situations what others see as problems by understanding that the only thing that you have to do is find the solution to this situation. Fear will always exist, like problems, differences, and between the black sheep and the rest is how they face them. We must be clear that just because they are brave does not mean that they are not afraid or that they do not face problems. The difference lies in how they face these situations; it is actually much simpler. From what most think, it is only about changing the approach. Generally, the approach is directed to the problem of fear.

For this reason, they cannot or find it very difficult to advance. Instead, the Black sheep focus their attention on the solution. Due to this simple change, they can dedicate their energy to face that situation that scares them or tackle that dreaded problem, giving the impression that they are not afraid of anything. Suppose the situation is that someone is unemployed. In that case, the white sheep focus on all the misfortunes that this implies, in addition to looking for someone or circumstance to blame for this fact, while the black sheep see this situation as an opportunity to change and improve. The focus and its energy are immediately directed to the search for a new job; By understanding this idea, regardless of the rest of the ideas discussed in this book, your life will have a drastically positive change. Therefore, you must dedicate yourself to finding solutions and stop focusing on which problems are to blame. This will help you face any situation that may arise without fear of any kind until this way of thinking or acting becomes a habit. Let us understand that we are all afraid of certain situations, but being afraid does not make it inferior or vulnerable. What really matters is how we choose to face and overcome our fears. With this simple change, you will begin to feel like a superman. or a super woman. In this way, they will begin to see him as that

THE CRITERIA OF THE SHEEP

person who, regardless of the magnitude of the situation, is capable of facing and solving it.

> *"Success is not final, failure is not fatal: what counts is the courage to continue."*
>
> **Winston Churchill**

CHAPTER 10
WELCOME TO THE BLACK SHEEP CLUB

BREAKING CHAINS

If you have reached this chapter, it is definitely because there is a black sheep that has already taken control or wants to take it within you. There is within you a voice, an energy, a force pushing you to do different things, to simply ask why? To look for different and more effective ways of doing things. Within you, you need to free yourself and break the chains that try to keep him imprisoned in a system or ideology that is no longer his. No greater reason fills me with pride and forces me to congratulate him by welcoming him to the black sheep club, our club, from now on: his club, which is made up of a select group of individuals who continually try to improve themselves regardless of the area in which they operate. I refer to those individuals who seek to improve themselves in various areas such as sports, health, physical condition, mental state, art, others, and whom I present my respect and admiration. However, at this point, I would like to address a group in particular, which is the one made up of those who are trying to improve themselves specifically in the financial area wanting and having as their final goal the much-desired financial freedom.

We live in a changing world, and if we do not manage to evolve and adapt to these changes, we are doomed to fail. Years ago,

THE CRITERIA OF THE SHEEP

many have confidence that the Government or the companies where they developed their careers would take care of them financially once they are working life ends. But this situation has drastically changed in recent years; that is, we cannot depend on third parties who, in one way or another, will take responsibility for us in financial matters when our working life ends. And if that is not the case, but if you are still working, the time will inevitably come when your production capacity will decrease, either due to your age or another reason, then, maintain the usual rhythm of life, that is, consumption to which you are accustomed, aggravated by the inevitable increase in health expenses, will generate an imbalance in your budget since your expenses will exceed your income, which, without a doubt, will put your wealth and the legacy of your family in imminent danger. In modern times you are solely responsible for your finances and therefore the only one who is responsible for managing them in the most efficient way. From these premises, I promote the idea that financial freedom should be the final goal that we set for ourselves at the beginning of our productive life.

Some think, right off the bat, that the term serves the simple purpose of accumulating as much wealth as possible, but that is not the goal or the way forward. There are those who defend the idea that the best way to achieve financial freedom is to live free of all debt, reducing your expenses as much as possible, which according to them, will improve your chances of living better when you retire with the little money you have managed to save. Those who defend this theory do not know or do not understand the concept of good debt and bad debt and, therefore, they believe that all debt is bad. I defend the idea that true wealth and, as a consequence, financial freedom are achieved through the accumulation or acquisition of assets (good debt) that generate income. In this way, your wealth will always be protected with the value of these assets since they will, in turn, generate the necessary cash flow for you to live in peace.

On the other hand, you have to be very careful to filter all the information that you will receive continuously as you will hear phrases such as: "Find what you really want to do and live on it", an extremely easy idea to sell but that most of the time does not apply to reality and if you apply it it will only serve you to "live on it." I think that the best thing is to produce money to be able to tackle the things that we really want to do. Regardless of what stage of your life you are in, you must understand that your goal has to be to achieve said financial freedom. Therefore, it is mandatory that you begin to think about how you are going to do it, visualize what you want, prepare yourself, educate yourself, design your work plan and start taking massive action on it.

OPTIONS

Only when you let your black sheep take full control will you then realize the infinite number of options that exist for you. We live in a world where more than 65% of individuals with a university degree work or practice in different areas to the one in which they graduated. I am such a case. Although I have a law degree, I have dedicated most of my productive life to sales and real estate. At 18, 19, or 20 years of age, it is often difficult to decide what we are going to do for the rest of our lives. I have realized, over time, that studying for a degree is no longer valid. And being someone is obviously a worthy achievement. But the truth is that you don't need a degree of any kind to add value or to make money in the modern world. Studying and preparing is vital, and education has to be continuous but directed to the area you want to practice in the specific case of sales, which is one of the areas that I am most passionate about. No degree is required. If you become a master in the area of negotiations and sales, the options and opportunities that you will have open will be endless, never the owner of a company in which you work, for example, real estate, will question you because you are selling too much since this translates into substantial income for both. Now, if you decide to start your own business, there is no doubt that

THE CRITERIA OF THE SHEEP

you are obliged, even more so, to know or to train in the area of sales.

Keep in mind that the many opportunities in the market are equivalent to the many and varied problems that exist in it. Being you a black sheep that has been formed in the area of negotiations, your nature and your ability to solve problems is still greater. So your options are not limited to any specific area, and you will be able to see clearly that we do not live in a world full of limitations, but on the contrary, you will begin to see and recognize all the options, all the opportunities that truly exist. In this way, you will be able to understand that we live in a world of abundance where there are no limits but those that you can set, only at this moment will your approach change completely, and you will stop looking for a certain area or a certain company since your gaze will be directed to the opportunities, no matter where they are, it is only in this moment that you will be able to grasp that the options are endless. Living in a world of abundance where the opportunities are endless, the options for success will also be, but only exclusively, when you decide to open your mind completely. Only then will you be able to see that all those options, options that have always been there, within your reach, waiting for you to you take advantage of them. Only in this moment will problems, unwanted situations, or obstacles become challenges, and you will always have the option of finding a way to face and overcome them. From now on, when you get a wall that prevents your progress, you will no longer stop at that point; you will instead accept the challenge and explore options to overcome that obstacle.

On the other hand, operating in this world will grant you countless options that you probably never had. Such as the ability to manage your own time, which is one of the things that I enjoy the most. In addition to what you achieve financially, you will have the option of doing all the things that give you enjoyment. Through time, I have known many who, upon achieving financial success, dedicate much of their time to fishing, practicing some sport, and participating in a music band, among many other activities. All these individuals managed to understand that you don't necessarily have to do what you love to live, do what makes you money so that you can then do what you like to do.

TO HELP

Keep in mind that when you are financially sound, you can definitely help many people. By this, I am not saying that you do not help anyone in their growth process. What I mean is to make you aware that the faster you reach your financial goals, the longer and more resources will have to collaborate or help everyone you want. It is like when you are going to travel on an airplane, and before this start, they indicate in the precautionary measures that in case of a problem and that the oxygen masks appear, first of all, put yours on before helping others due to that if you lose consciousness, regardless of your good intentions, you will not be able to help anyone else. Giving back, sharing, or helping is a gratifying experience, and it is within everyone's reach to put it into practice at any time. There are those who try to deceive themselves by repeating phrases over and over again, such as: "The day I have money, I am going to do such a thing to help someone," keep in mind that giving is not limited solely to money, so regardless of your financial situation giving or helping is always within your reach, money like alcohol works as a magnifying glass and helps you to really see who is who, helping is a good habit that we have to develop at all times of our lives, being aware that when we reach our financial goal, we will be able to help many more with time or money.

All this is part of the nature of the black sheep; that is why you see those who have managed to accumulate great wealth helping those who need it most in a massive way, either by promoting scholarships for studies, helping to feed the neediest, creating or

THE CRITERIA OF THE SHEEP

supporting different types of foundations, or simply donating time or money for specific causes with the sole purpose of having a positive impact on the community, as I mentioned before. I repeat it again because of its importance, you have the power to help others at any time according to your possibilities, and as you grow older, you can undoubtedly increase your contributions. When you reach the top of your aspirations for no reason, forget your roots, much less the help you may have received or received at some point in your life from friends, family, clients, strangers, or anyone else who in one way or another has helped you get to where you are, recognizing the help received along the way will not detract from your achievements, therefore, you should always give credit to it. It is up to everyone who deserves it.

There are many ways in which you can collaborate and have a positive impact on society, even beyond time or money. By being part of the select group of black sheep, you will become a leader in both your business. On a social level, simply sharing your experience and knowledge could positively impact and set an example for many others. If by now you have not yet begun to collaborate or help in one way or another those around you or, beyond that, society in general, it is good that you start doing so; If you do not feel it necessary at this time, do not worry, the need will come as it is in the nature of the black sheep to help others, this is the true law of attraction. The more you give, the more you receive, if you want good things to happen, go out and do good things, I can guarantee you that the feeling of well- being will be sufficient payment for everything you are doing, social consciousness has evolved to such a point that it has created an unprecedented movement in which you can see every more and more individual are coming together to create positive social impacts. You have to be a part of such a wonderful cause.

TIME

Time, without a doubt, is the most important asset, the most valuable asset that we all have; the good news is that regardless of who you are, we all have the same time, and it will only depend on us how we manage it, from any day on of the year we all have a year ahead that consists of 12 months and 365days of 24 hours each. All weeks have 7 days and all hours 60 minutes. In other words, time does not discriminate; therefore, we all have the same amount of time to do our things. Only by being clear about this will you be able to realize that the popular phrase "I don't have time to do that" is nothing more than an excuse to which we go every time we want to justify why we have not done any activity. Keep in mind that you are the owner of your own time, so you are in control of it; According to statistics, the successful ones sleep 6 to 8 hours a day, followed by another group made up mostly of white sheep that sleep 8 to 10 hours a day and even more, what is striking is that this second group is the one that generally does not have time to do anything else, does not have time to do anything extra and simply its members fall into a vicious cycle of complaining about not having time, not realizing that the simple adjustment of waking up 2 hours earlier. Every day I would give them 14 extra hours a week, approximately 56 extra hours a month and 670 hours a year, time that they could invest in some important project without having to modify their lives drastically. You, as a black sheep, will understand this and will take full control of your time.

I remember once, one Sunday, that I was working and a friend told me in a somewhat reproachful tone: "Well, if you work on Sundays then what day do you spend spending time with your family," with a smile I replied: " Every day "and then I explained to him that for some reason society imposed that Sunday is the day to dedicate to the family, a thought that seems a bit selfish to me since why dedicate a single day to it when you can dedicate all of them. The point is that this is possible only when you own

THE CRITERIA OF THE SHEEP

your time, which means that you can take a Wednesday off to take your children to the park or a Monday off to take your parents to lunch, in this way 7 days of the week have no difference. In the white sheep society, Monday is the worst day of the week for having to go back to work, but in the black sheep world, Mondays, like any other day, are exciting as they represent a new opportunity to advance and improve if you did not understand this concept it is of the utmost importance that you take your time to understand it and you will realize that there are ways that you can own your own time, as you could, equally, be the owner of your company achieving financial freedom, among other options. It is mandatory that you start to manage your time in the best possible way, consider going to bed an hour earlier, getting up an hour or two earlier, analyze how much time you spend watching television, how much time you spend on social networks, or how much time you spend on the Internet just watching programs or videos that perhaps do not teach you anything, we live in a world of information where computers or cell phones, among others, give us access to the Internet and all the information that exists in that network, the only thing left for us is to know how to filter in what type of information we are going to invest time, this simple adjustment could create a great positive impact on your life. You must understand the importance of time, and in this way, you will be more aware of how you invest it, learn at once to say "No" to minor activities that do not make you happy or that do not bring you closer to your goals, this is a highly recommended practice which one never finishes learning and which one must constantly try to improve.

LUCK WILL ALWAYS BE ON YOUR SIDE
The moment you decide to be yourself and behave differently from what is considered socially normal, you have complete assurance that you will be judged, at first they may label you as crazy or, failing that, they will criticize your actions by qualifying

them as lo- priests, which in the end is the same; This happens because they generally do not understand the change in attitude, I mean that they do not understand how to go outside the established patterns of behavior considered by society as normal. If you manage to overcome this stage of criticism and attacks, you will see, as you continue advancing, that a fascinating phenomenon will occur, as it succeeds, most will attribute this achievement to an external factor: luck should not take personally. This type of attack, I mean do not give credit for your achievements, understand that all these individuals who belong to the white sheep society attribute their failures and frustrations to external factors such as the Government, the economy, the weather, the lack of opportunity, the time or the moment, among many others, without understanding what to overcome and reach their success does not depend on anything or anyone outside you, but on yourself, for this reason, they do not understand that you decided to put yourself in this situation, the success or improvement achieved is the product of your decision and effort, for the simple fact of not understanding this is that they attribute their success to luck and the more successful it is, it will be justified with phrases such as: "He is very lucky," creating the illusion that luck is always on your side without understanding that you are the creator of your own luck.

From my point of view, luck depends on a set of factors that includes: being positive, visualization, preparation or education, action, evolution, adaptation, and consistency; Only when all these factors come together does the possibility of luck begin to exist and the more you work or, the more you apply these resources, the luckier you will be. Only when we accept that we are the makers of our luck is when we will be able to understand that hope is not a strategy, that just hoping or hoping to be lucky will not bring any kind of result until you do something to make things happen, it is then when can they happen. The road to success is not as easy a route as we initially imagined. I assure

THE CRITERIA OF THE SHEEP

you that it will be full of problems, situations, ups and downs, obstacles, challenges, and, in general, many adversities. Only by staying focused, committed, and constant will we overcome and overcome all these situations. This will seem to the white sheep that it is a matter of luck. In truth, the only determining factor for this to happen is derived from hard and persevering work. Neither luck, faith, nor hope can guarantee the results that you will get when you really work hard to achieve what you want. Failing a few attempts does not mean you failed, losing a battle does not mean you lost the war, much less does it mean you are out of luck. Every time we fall, get up and go back. In trying, we will be forging our own luck.

Let us remember that everything begins with an idea, followed by the vision or visualization of its materialization. At this moment, we allow ourselves to begin to change our luck, always keeping in mind that if we want to have the same luck that everyone has, we just have to behave as the great majority behave. Only and exclusively when we think, act, and, in general, are different, we will be able to opt for what many call good luck. Therefore, you are the only one who will have the power to decide whether or not you will have good luck since you only responsible and creator of it, the more he works in his dreams or in his goals and the more you advance in your journey to success, the more you will generate the illusion that you are a being that always has luck on your side.

THE POTENTIAL EARNINGS ARE INFINITE

Once you manage to free your mind, it will be when you can expand your horizons; then you will realize that we live in a world where the possibilities are infinite. For this reason, the potential gains are infinite; when you finish with the mentality of the poor, which is full of scarce thoughts, it is then you will be able to see clearly everything that this world and this life offers, and that is when you realize that all these opportunities are within your reach, that it is not up to anyone to go out and get what you deserve so much, and it is not anyone's fault, but yourself, that until now you have not had what you have wanted. Understand that greed does not mean anything other than wanting more, and wanting more has nothing wrong. On the contrary, wanting more is synonymous with self-improvement, but this idea is not fully approved in the society of white sheep. Therefore, many times they give a negative sense to greed, only when the black sheep takes control will it be given realize that wanting more to aspire to improve in any area has nothing wrong, this obviously applies to the financial field in which understanding that there is nothing wrong in wanting more. That we live in a world of abundance and therefore the potential gains are infinite, it is imperative that we go out to search and try to obtain everything that we believe we are capable of obtaining, being clear that what we put in our mind will become our reality, by expanding our horizons we will understand that everything that is out there is within our grasp.

Only when you, the black sheep, take absolute control will you finally understand that we live in a world of abundance in which there are no limits, and then you will break the chains that keep you tied to the ideology that limits exist. Resources are scarce, thoughts and beliefs that come from a society full of limitations. Yes, for this at times, there is still an existential conflict within you in which you debate whether it is true that we live in a world of scarcity or abundance, in which, on the one hand, something tells you that it is okay where it is for being a safe place and on the other hand something tells you to go out and find what is within your reach since you may have more than you currently have; In other words: if the white sheep that is inside you is justifying why you cannot move forward, because you do not deserve it and that it is better that you stay where you are for reasons of security and stability. Feeding all the excuses and fears to that in this way, it is not logical to want to do something different. On the other hand, the black sheep tells you that

THE CRITERIA OF THE SHEEP

moving forward, adapting and evolving is in your genes, that you deserve and that everything you really want is within your reach, that you are a creative and innovative being, a brave being and, therefore, you are not afraid of anything, that wanting to advance and improve yourself is something necessary for your internal well-being, that there is nothing wrong with thinking differently, in acting different and in general, in being different, and that advancement and personal progress constitute a moral obligation; If this duality of criteria is the conflict you are experiencing, then you must obey and impose your status as a black sheep that you have decided to assume as a member of our club and act accordingly.

So, the next question would be: if we live in a world of abundance in which there are no limits, how much success could you be? The direct answer is: there are no limits to success, and you, at this moment, are capable of achieving it and understand that since the potential gains are infinite, having no limits, the success of others will not affect in any way your ability to be successful as well. Success itself is intangible. It is not physical, which means that it is something that cannot be inherited, bought, or demanded. It is something that we must achieve for ourselves and for ourselves, let us understand once, and for all that success it is not limited to time and much less to place and that the simple fact that we decide to move forward puts us in a situation of improvement which automatically transforms or translates into success. Therefore, when we give the first step automatically, you will become a successful person, and only you can decide how many steps you will advance or how far you want to go on your way to success.

FINAL THOUGHTS
We live in a world where there is the illusion that a set of external factors limit or prevent us from improving ourselves, where the fear of doing something different is transmitted and spread from generation to generation, where society has created

a series of parameters of the which we cannot get out of if we want to lead a normal life. But also, there has always been a group that has never agreed with this ideology, a group of individuals who have dared to separate from the herd, who have dared to ask Why? Who dared to ask, is there a better way? Who have dared to think, act, and, in general, to be different, individuals who have dared to break with all these barriers created by a society that often does not seem to have its own criteria or that is still tied to rigid ways of thinking or beliefs from other times? This group, initially described as crazy, is made up of all those who, later on, society itself would identify as geniuses.

The moment you decide to join this group since we all can do it. Since we all have the same opportunity, the only thing you need is that you permit yourself to do it. If you want to achieve different results, you have to behave differently from the rest, only when we understand that we can do it is when we will allow ourselves to advance, to progress, in order to begin our path of improvement in the area or areas that only you can identify as important in your life, always bearing in mind that nothing is impossible when we believe in ourselves since, as I said, we all have the same capacity and the same opportunities because we live in a world of abundance, this is an open invitation to all those who, at some point, they were called or treated like black sheep to join a select group that is characterized, among many other things, by the desire to succeed and overcome Go continuously on a personal level.

ABOUT THE AUTHOR

Víctor Baptista lives in Orlando, Florida, in the USA. He remains an active investor in the real estate area as well as an entrepreneur or businessman in the real estate market, graduated

THE CRITERIA OF THE SHEEP

as a lawyer in his country of origin, Venezuela, came as an immigrant to the US.

Looking for new opportunities. Without speaking the language, he started his first job as a dishwasher, but always aware of all the opportunities that existed around him, he worked as a cashier in a gas station, installing ceramics or earthenware, laying bricks in patios, as a gardener, until who found a way to start his first business.

After forming and selling two successful companies, he begins his adventure in the real estate world by awakening this great passion never before experienced with any of his other businesses. He identifies this matter as the area to which he wants to dedicate his life and his race. Now, with experience in multiple real estate's areas such as the acquisition, remodeling, and sale of properties (flip), the planning, construction, and sale of both single-family and multi-family homes, the evaluation, acquisition, and sale of properties that produce a flow of cash, among others, is currently actively participating in the real estate market.

Always taking into consideration how difficult it is to take the first step, he has dedicated part of his time to transmitting his knowledge to others. In this sense, he decides to write his first book: Real Estate Secrets, in order to have more scope and achieve that your message reaches as many people as possible; Following this idea, he writes his second book to communicate such a simple message to everyone, which is: "With the correct ideology, it can be done."

To order more copies, please visit: www.amazon.com

Finally, if this book has inspired you, the best thing you can do is transmit such energy to others, let them know about the existence of the book, and help them take that very difficult first step.

www.ingramcontent.com/pod-product-compliance
Lightning Source LLC
Chambersburg PA
CBHW070646220526
45466CB00001B/314